The ABC's of
EFFECTIVE PARENTING

Supervising Character Formation in Children

✦

Gresham Royal Holton, *Ph.D.*

PUBLISHED BY

Growing Panes

3543 Raintree Drive   Valdosta, Georgia 31601

The ABC's of EFFECTIVE PARENTING
Supervising Character Formation in Children

Copyright © 2016 Gresham Royal Holton
grholton@yahoo.com

ISBN: 0990549941
ISBN-13:978-0-9905499-4-9

Printed by CreateSpace, An Amazon.com Company

Available from Amazon.com, CreateSpace.com, and other retail outlets

2016

DEDICATED TO

RAINTREE VILLAGE BOARDS OF DIRECTORS

(1980 – 2015)

My respect has continued to grow for the men and women who serve and have served on this board over the past thirty-plus years. They serve for no other reason but that they love children. They assume a great legal liability and responsibility as unpaid volunteers. Were it not for them, this book would probably not have been written.

I especially want to hold in honor the following men who served during the early days of my work at Raintree Village: Harry Dennard, Harry Talbott, Billy Schroer, Emory McCullough, Gene Russell, Lewis Stewart, Joel Johnson, Nilas Manley, Bill Harvey, Tom Parris, Richard Boyd, Earl O'Neal, Gordon Teffeteller, Dan Osburn and Warren Shaw. They were particularly encouraging.

Actually, this book is dedicated to all the men and women serving on child care boards who commit their time, their talents, and their money to partner with the natural parents to form character in needy children.

Gresham R. Holton

Preface

"Character!" What is it?

Mrs. Sapp came into my office again with the same complaint, "He again has refused to make up his bed!" referring to one of the 14-year old boys in her care. Rightly so, she was concerned that his act of defiance would encourage others to rebel. Yet, with a smile, she almost admired his defiance.

Another example of how to strengthen the emerging resilience of character, while disciplining the disobedient act! How to channel the energy generated by the defiance into the "grit" that caused him to stand up in the first place! Odd as it sounds, an act of disobedience in a child is a wonderful opportunity to think past the moment to see that child becoming a world-changing leader.

> Grit in turnip greens may just ruin a good meal, but in the bearings of a fine-tuned machine it is highly destructive! We gauge sandpaper and grindstones in terms of "grit" ...the ability to stand up against resistance!

At Raintree Village *True Grit* is that inner decision-making framework of traits we call "character". Grit, or basic character, is the dynamic process by which we decide to stand up against adversity, correct social wrongs, and recover from individual failures. Words such as "backbone", "metal", "strong-willed" are used to describe it!

We believe in *"True"* grit! *Resistance* to immoral conduct and destructive habits. Everyone loses when lying is socially acceptable and sexual experiences have no boundaries.

Raintree Village is in the business of building character. Every aspect of our work focuses on helping a young person gain independence, the freedom to act responsibly.

Our example: At the early age of twelve Jesus "stood up" (Luke 2) against the abuses and false notions of His day. His parents saw it as an act of disobedience. It was *true grit* of the highest order. This growth continued, and *"Jesus grew in wisdom and stature, and in favor with God and man* (Luke 2:52)."

<u>Wisdom</u>, <u>stature</u>, <u>favor with God</u> and <u>man</u>! This sentence captures the mission of Raintree Village *to supervise* the formation of character in our children. We want our children to grow to be strong adults with ***True Grit!***

-Gresham Royal Holton

Contents

Preface:
"Character!" What is it?

Acknowledgments
Foreword
Introduction

Prologue:
Open Letter to Parenting Supervisors   1

PART 1: PARENTING SUPERVISION PRINCIPLES

Chapter One:
RELATIONSHIPS: The Core of Parenting   3

Chapter Two:
ACCEPTABLE: Standards of Character   15

Chapter Three:
BEHAVIORS: Defining Right Conduct   37

Chapter Four:
CHOICES: Training to Choose Wisely   53

PART 2: A PRACTICAL APPLICATION

Chapter Five:
ABC'S: Acceptable Behaviors Choices   65

Chapter Six:
CONDUCT LEVELS: Setting the Standards   81

Chapter Seven:
    M-O-M REPORT: Right Conduct Choices   99

PART 3: REAL CHARACTER FORMATION

Chapter Eight:
    DISCIPLINE: Not Discourage   115

Chapter Nine:
    DANGER: Child Abuse   139

Chapter Ten:
    CHANGE: A Lifetime Challenge   149

Chapter Eleven:
    CHARACTER: The *Finished Product*   163

Epilogue:
    JESUS: The Ideal Model   179

APPENDIX: 187
    Case Studies Examples (by Jackie Parker, *MS)*
    Form 1: Child's Likes/Dislikes Survey
    Form 2: Mode of Maintenance (MOM) Report
    Form 3: Staffing Meetings
    Form 4: Supervision and Conduct Levels

RESOURCES   203

Acknowledgements

It is not possible to acknowledge everyone who has had a part in developing this book. Dozens of staff members at Raintree Village have contributed ideas and applications to these principles in training meetings over more than thirty years. Hundreds of children have literally experienced the process in their day-to-day living under the *Acceptable Behaviors Choices* supervision system.

The principles have been taught in family life conferences in several churches and professional conferences. Both natural parents and professional parenting supervisors have given valuable feedback on child development issues.

Pam Webb Dasher initiated the research on the "differences in problem children and model children" while completing a degree at Valdosta State University in the 1980's. Her research became the basis for the child preference survey.

Jackie Parker, Programs Director at Raintree Village, has supervised the ABC applications for many years. She has also written the Case Studies in the Appendix that pertain to actual children.

Toni Holton Webb, a mother and grandmother, has read and edited the manuscript. As a skilled writer, she has provided invaluable advice in the literary composition. In addition, she had first-hand knowledge as a child of many of the principles of this book.

I've learned a lot from my dear wife, our five children's mother, who is the most accomplished parenting supervisor I know. She is a model of two of the critical elements in effective parenting – *fairness* and *flexibility!* Her parenting style is both strict and loving. She mirrors strong traits of character that she must have gotten from her parents, and she has that unique ability to keep on keeping on when times get tough. Sharlene knows that supervising the formation of character in children is hard work, --but it is worth it all!

Foreword

⚜

In a time where broken families abound, this book provides a clear guide for teaching, learning, and healing. Though this book speaks to parents, this book is a must have for any person seeking guidance in working professionally with children. It expounds upon the importance of relationships and values, adventuring into helping children develop character by learning to manage their own behaviors. This book provides a practical approach for those Dr. Holton calls "parenting supervisors" in how to develop inner strength in children.

As someone who believes that one of the highest callings of all Christians is to care for children, I appreciate the principles of this book. It not only defines effective parenting in the natural family, but also advocates for the sincere importance in caring for *all* children. It lends itself to the resilience that children and families are built upon. Parenting, particularly for professional parenting supervisors is not for the weak or faint of heart. It is an endeavor that requires the utmost respect and effort.

Dr. Holton highlights the essence of parenting when he states, "the deeds we do are stronger for our children than the words we say."

The first chapters of the book lay the foundation of how the child care supervisors' values permeate a child's identity.

The daily interactions between supervisors with character and the children under their supervision is the process for character building. The repetitive choices a child makes, under the supervision of the parents, evolve around core values. This evolution drives the choices made by the children with various rewards and restrictions, and thus promotes the formation of character.

How, and under what conditions and values these principles operate is the heart of the system.

The latter chapters are allocated to a system of professional child care based on the foregoing principles, a system that has been tried and proven true. It works!

How it works at Raintree Village is offered as an example and model for other child care programs, including child care in the natural family. A few practical case studies of actual examples of *how it works* are provided in the *Appendix.*

Jackie Parker, *MS*
Director of Social Services
Raintree Village Children and Family Services, Inc.

Introduction

The ABC's of Effective Parenting presents a training process for supervisors of children, including natural parents. The *process* involves how to instill the abilities in children to make *good* behavior choices. It is not presented to train children, but to train the supervisors of children. The narrow focus of the training equips parenting supervisors to teach children to make behavior choices that will improve their qualities of life in the community where they live.

The ABC system *does not* address many of the qualities and practices that are evident in effective parenting. For example, important variables like natural family history are not considered. In a traditional natural family many of the family rules and policies are mutually developed over time. The ABC system is a *process* approach designed to equip a child with effective decision-making skills for any situation in life. Although much is said about the *content of character*, the main focus is on *how* that content became a part of character.

The importance of effective parenting, or supervising the training of children is clearly defined in the words of the wise man Solomon:

> "*Train up a child in the way he should go, and when he is old he will not depart from it.*" (Proverbs 22:7).

The key words in this injunction are "should go". This implies that parents are to instill in children the abilities to survive for a lifetime. What is that? We call it "spunk" or "grit" or "character!" *Character* is that framework of strengths which makes us strong, composed of the historical experiences of our choices. . . the very core of our being! At the heart of character are the good choices we have made in life. Training a child to make good choices in life springs from the basic values instilled. Values determine direction!

Thus this series of lessons focuses on *how those values of character are formed* in a child through the "training" provided by the child's supervisors, or parents. The approach uses family systems theory as a model. The basic standards proposed are the traditional values of middle American Christianity. However, our purpose is not to promote the "content" of the training, but the "process" of how it happens.

Training children is serious business! What supervisor of a child has not agonized over this injunction! Many parents suffer enduring guilt many years after their children are grown because of their feelings of failure in parenting. Professional child care supervisors seek ways to improve their methods and help in doing their jobs better. *Training children is serious business!*

The ABC's of Effective Parenting describes one approach to fulfilling this important process. This is a day-to-day approach to how parents can form *character* in a child. The "Acceptable Behavior Choices" System has been developed over five decades in training children both as a father in the natural biological family, and as a professional Christian child care worker in a residential child care community.

The first four chapters define the "unit" of this series of lessons in terms of relationships. The parent-child relationship is the core organization of a family. More children and other adults make the relationship unit even more complex. *Real* character is the product of children's interactions in their formative years with the adults who supervised them, and significant others in their intimate world.

Chapters five through seven describe how "the ABC System" works in a professional child care facility. This detailed illustration and application of the principles in an actual professional child care facility can help natural family parents see the results that are possible. The "Acceptable Behaviors Choices" System has been the conduct training model used in Raintree Village Children's Home programs for more than three decades.

Chapters eight and nine focus on how discipline is both a blessing and a danger. Discipline is the process that supports the values and corrects the behaviors of a child. This is where "the rubber hits the road!" But, it is also the point of greatest danger of abusing the child.

The final two chapters are clarions of hope. The work of forming character takes a lifetime. In most cases there are opportunities for "do-overs!"

The final chapter is our feeble attempt to describe the *finished product!* "Character" is an elusive composite of a person's values, choices, behaviors, and the resulting visible traits...over a lifetime! It is difficult to visualize a *finished product.* Yet, the parenting supervisor must have a clear vision of it, and be able to transfer that vision to the child.

An Epilogue is added to our study to provide the real baseline standard for all Christian parenting supervisors. It is an example from the life of Jesus Christ when he was just twelve years old. Our case for "acceptable choices" could be outlined by this Bible example. I contend, without apology, that Jesus Christ is the model that sets the standards.

The overall purpose of this study is to help sincere, good-character-supervisors of children be more effective in building that same character in their charges! We do not want to make parents feel guiltier about their duties as parents than they already do. We do propose a plan for more effective parenting supervision that has proven to have good results.

The *Appendix* contains samples of the *forms* developed for use in a professional child care facility. They may be adapted for use in a professional child care agency or a traditional family setting. Several actual *case studies* from Raintree Village are provided to illustrate the ABC principles in practice.

Our ultimate goal is to save children by instilling the core character they need to survive in a changing hostile world!

Prologue:

An Open Letter to Parenting Supervisors

Throughout this study I have purposely used the term "parenting supervisors" rather than "child care supervisors", "child caregivers" or even just "parents." This is due to two very important reasons.

First, many children are placed in family situations other than the natural family. These supervisors are charged, often by law and regulation, with the responsibilities of natural parents. In fact, these "out-of-home" parental supervisors are often held to an even higher standard today than natural parents. In addition, many natural families are far different from just a few years ago. Children are supervised in single-parent families, both-parents-working families as well as the traditional "mom-dad-and-the-kids" families. Yet, many other children spend their entire childhood in "out-of-home" supervision living in group homes and foster homes.

The second reason is because of the basic purpose for parenting, which is supervising the growth of children to become adults. While their physical bodies are developing, their minds are also evolving from the dependent lack of wisdom of youth to the independent ability to stand alone. Parenting is to help the developing person grow to adulthood physically, mentally and spiritually. This study focuses on *how* the structure of "character" is developed in a child by the natural parents or by other parenting supervisors. I have chosen to define this ability, or mental framework to make good behavior choices in life as "character." Character may also be defined as the composite "grit" composed of heart held values and time tested experiences of those values in action over time.

Supervising the development of character in children is arguably the most important thing you could ever do. Your work will affect our world for years to come. You are contributing to the leadership of our nation. Parental supervisors are critically important! It may sound like just a cliché, but *"character matters!"* That is what this is about. You are the key that opens the minds and hearts of the next generation of adults. You are instrumental in helping them develop the inner strength they will need to scale the mountains of the future. Your acts of parental supervision must be both a mission and a ministry.

Make the commitment to do the best you can. But accept the fact that the character independence you instill in your children results from *their* choices, --rather than yours! Never fall into the habit of beating yourself up because of the poor choices they make!

Thus, your final role as a parenting supervisor is to respect your children by allowing them to make their own mistakes and perhaps, to suffer the consequences. Yet, you maintain your integrity by modeling a life before them that accurately reflects your values. Be genuine.

That's the gift you give that will last! The first *PARENTING SUPERVISION PRINCIPLE* could be: **Do the best you can do and leave the rest to God!**

Chapter One

⋅⟨◈⟩⋅

RELATIONSHIPS:
The Core Unit

PARENTING SUPERVISION PRINCIPLES

1   *Parenting supervisors should establish and maintain a healthy attachment with a child to facilitate character formation.*

2   *A healthy relationship between parenting supervisors and a child must include trust, love and mutual support.*

3   *The inner structure of character is developed in the small routine daily family interaction behaviors.*

"Life is relationships!" could be Bob Bryant's motto. Bob, the father of four grown children of high character, ends just about every email with this phrase in bold letters. Relationships of all kinds do help mold our lives into the kinds of people we become. Our families provide the pros and cons, the helps and hurts, that contribute to our social development. On the other hand, aborted or unhealthy relationships could describe the dysfunction of too many American families where isolation and abandonment reign. Broken homes resulting in more single-parent families are not only prime examples of the

demise of the family, but they also encourage other unhealthy relationships.

The relationship interactions between parents and children, supervisors and trainees, and mentors and disciples form the framework for developing character. A relationship is the platform from which appropriate performances in life develop. Forming healthy relationships begins early, and continues for many years, if not for an entire lifetime. Forming, molding, and maintaining these close ties also incubate the individual traits of character.

If we lack character, our lives are lived in a void. As always, the children seem to suffer the most in such cases. Many children have been deprived of the basic nurturing they needed.

Such children may have experienced tremendous loss of parents, home, and friends in a divorce or incarceration crisis. These children may have "lost faith" in everyone and everything due to their significant relationship experiences.

"Disconnected children" are the lost souls of our world. Each one represents a story of failure in developing and maintaining an anchor of stable basic character. Isolated, these children often turn to the deviant-culture world of drugs, gangs, and immorality. In view of this loss to our world, it is appropriate to begin a study of how to supervise the formation of character by describing the human bonding of building healthy relationships.

NEGATIVE NON-RELATIONSHIPS

First, we must identify what is missing in disconnected children. Two words describe what they have lost: *attachment* and *bonding*. The clinical name for this developmental malady is Reactive Attachment Disorder (RAD). Although similar, *attachment* and *bonding* are not the same.   *Bonding* occurs when a parent meets the child's needs, consistently and in a timely manner. For example, even a wild animal can be trained to eat out of your hand if you bring food consistently in a timely manner. However, the animal does not become attached. *Attachment* is the emotional bond that grows over time between the parents and the child. It results from many factors including *trust, feelings of affection, and met needs.* At the center of both emotions and needs satisfaction is mutual *trust.*

In 1958, British developmental psychologist John Bowlby published the ground-breaking paper "The Nature of the Child's Tie to his Mother," in which the concepts of attachment theory were developed. The theory of *emotional bond* is based on the universal tendency for humans to attach, i.e. to seek closeness to another person and to feel secure when that person is present. This is the basic motivation for building relationships.

Attachment is the deep connection established between a child and the parenting supervisors that profoundly affects the child's development and ability to express emotions and develop relationships.

Any child can grow up with problems of attachment, but adopted and foster children are particularly at risk. Children with attachment disorders or other attachment problems have difficulty connecting to others and managing their own emotions.

There are several common signs and symptoms of reactive attachment disorder (RAD).

An aversion to touch and physical affection.

Children with reactive attachment disorder often flinch, laugh, or even say "Ouch" when touched. Rather than producing positive feelings, touch and affection are perceived as a threat.

Control issues.

Most children with reactive attachment disorder go to great lengths to remain in control and avoid feeling helpless. They are often disobedient, defiant, and argumentative.

Anger problems.

Anger may be expressed directly, in tantrums or acting out, or through manipulative, passive-aggressive behavior. Children with reactive attachment disorder may hide their anger in socially acceptable actions, like giving a high five that hurts or hugging someone too hard.

Difficulty showing genuine care and affection.

For example, children with reactive attachment disorder may act inappropriately affectionate with strangers while displaying little or no affection towards their parents.

An underdeveloped conscience.

Children with reactive attachment disorder may act like they don't have a conscience and fail to show guilt, regret, or remorse after behaving badly.

As a child grows older, by early teens, the disorder may take one of two symptomatic profiles:

1) *Inhibited symptoms of reactive attachment disorder* (RAD). The child is extremely withdrawn, emotionally detached, and resistant to comforting. The child is aware of what's going on around him or her, even hyper-vigilant, but doesn't react or respond. He or she may push others away, ignore them, or even act out in aggression when others try to get close.

2) *Disinhibited symptoms of reactive attachment disorder* (RAD). The child doesn't seem to prefer his

or her parents over other people, even strangers. The child seeks comfort and attention from virtually anyone, without distinction. He or she is extremely dependent, acts much younger than his or her age, and may appear chronically anxious.

A HEALTHY RELATIONSHIP

Clues for healthy relationships between a parenting supervisor and a child can be seen in an opposite description of reactive attachment disorders symptoms:

Openness to physical touching.

It is healthy for parents and children to appropriately touch each other.   This behavior encapsulates the connections a child needs.   Plus, it also manifests an ability to show emotions.

Respect for the boundaries

Especially the boundaries between the parents and the child! In child abuse cases, this would mean knowing the difference in a "good touch" and a "bad touch". Healthy relationships have clearly defined boundaries for each individual involved.   Whereas the "emotional" touching is physical, understanding the boundaries is more rational.

Recognize the values of being the parent or the child.

The parents must be "parents" and a child will be "a child" based on their inherent core values (next chapter). Our values are "built in" by someone at an earlier age. Our core values guide our responses to others.   They must be identified and clearly defined between the supervisor and the child.

Resolve any differences through mutual communications.

In a healthy relationship the parents take the initiative to stimulate self-disclosure, *the talking cure*. At the same time, the recognition and respect noted above will prevail. Developing relationships tests our abilities to solve interaction problems.

HEALTHY PARENTAL ATTACHMENT

Do not add to the stress the child is already feeling by your own obvious stress. The "detachment" the child feels is the scary feeling of being all alone. All children seek to be attached, connected in a very special way with other people, especially their parenting supervisors. A healthy attachment must be established and maintained to provide the platform for healthy character formation. How can you, as the child's supervisor, help the child form such attachments?

BUILD TRUST

First, continually remind yourself that this is a matter of *T-R-U-S-T!* Your objective is to help the child learn *how* to trust! That takes time. But, there are some things you can do to help them.

Be realistic in your expectations.

Helping your child with an attachment disorder may require a lot of time and effort. Focus on making small steps forward and then celebrate every sign of success.

Be patience.

The process may not be as rapid as you'd like, and you can expect bumps along the way. But by remaining patient and focusing on small improvements, you create an atmosphere of safety for your child.

Safety is the core issue for children with attachment problems. They are distant and distrustful because they feel unsafe in the world. They keep their guards up to protect themselves, but it also prevents them from accepting love and support. So before anything else, it is essential to build up your child's sense of security. You can accomplish this by establishing clear expectations and rules of behavior. Your consistent responses to their behaviors is very important. The child will soon learn that he or she can predict what you will do in any given situation. Thus, your interactions teach the child that he or she can depend on you.

Set limits and boundaries.

Consistent, loving boundaries make the world seem more predictable and less scary to children with attachment problems such as reactive attachment disorder. It is important that they understand what behavior is expected of them, what is and is not acceptable, and what the consequences will be if they disregard the rules. This also teaches them that they have more control over what happens to them than they think.

Take charge, yet remain calm when your child is upset or misbehaving.

Remember that "bad" behavior means that your child does not know how to handle what he or she is feeling and needs your help. By staying calm, you show your child that the feeling is manageable. Never discipline a child with an attachment disorder when you're in an emotionally-charged state. This makes the child feel more unsafe and may even reinforce the bad behavior.

Such children want to be in control. You give them control when they learn they can *push your buttons* and you will react!

Be immediately available to reconnect following a conflict.

Conflict can be especially disturbing for children with insecure attachment or attachment disorders. After a conflict or tantrum where you have had to discipline your child, be ready to reconnect as soon as he or she is ready. This reinforces your consistency and love, and will help your child develop trust that you will be there for them.

Own up to mistakes.

When you let frustration or anger get the best of you or you do something you realize is insensitive, quickly address the mistake. Your willingness to take responsibility and make amends can strengthen the attachment bond.

Try to maintain predictable routines and schedules.

A child with an attachment disorder will not rely on loved ones for directions. A familiar routine or schedule can provide comfort during times of change.

DEMONSTRATE LOVE

Second, a child who has not bonded early in life will have a hard time accepting love, especially physical expressions of love. Love is actually built on foundations of trust. But you can help them learn to accept your love with time, consistency, and repetition. Trust and security come from seeing loving actions, hearing reassuring words, and feeling comforted over and over again. It is nearly impossible to train in love without trust, or trust without love! These two active traits are essential in completing the process of forming character in a child.

Find things that feel good to your child.

If possible, show your love through rocking, cuddling, and holding—attachment experiences he or she missed out on earlier. But always be respectful of what feels comfortable and good to your child. In cases of previous abuse and trauma, you may have to go very slowly because your child may be very resistant to physical touch.

Respond to your child's emotional age.

Children with attachment disorders often act like younger children, both socially and emotionally. You may need to treat them as though they were much younger, using more non-verbal methods of soothing and comforting.

Help your child identify emotions and express his or her needs.

Children with attachment disorders may not know what they are feeling or how to ask for what they need. Reinforce the idea that all feelings are okay and show them healthy ways to express their emotions.

Listen, talk, and play with your child.

Carve out times when you are able to give your child your full, focused attention in ways that feel comfortable to him or her. It may seem hard to drop everything, eliminate distractions, and just be in the moment, but quality time together provides a great opportunity.

PROVIDE SUPPORT

Third, among the things that build relationships, the routine activities of a family are the most significant. Most such activities center on the normal health-needs of a child. A child's eating, sleep, and exercise habits along with other daily routines are very important in building healthy relationships. Healthy lifestyle habits can go a long way in reducing your child's stress levels and leveling out mood swings. When children with attachment disorders are relaxed, well-rested, and feeling good, it will be much easier for them to handle life's challenges.

Eating

Make sure your child eats healthy which would include a diet full of whole grains, fruits, vegetables, and lean protein. A plus is for the family to eat together. Mealtime is an excellent time for bonding.

Sleep

Sleep deprivation can cause your child to be tired during the day. A tired child has a harder time learning new things. Make your child's sleep schedule (bed-time and wake time) consistent. Use this routine to provide structure and control.

Exercise

Exercise or any type of physical activity triggers endorphins and gives your child a sense of well-being. Exercise can be a great antidote to stress, frustration, and pent-up emotion. Physical activity is especially important for the angry child.

Daily Routines

Yes, even daily chores can attach a child to the supervisor. One of the signs of a dysfunctional relationship between a child and a parent is when the child actually does something wrong in order to get the parents attention...even if it includes discipline!

Discussion Questions:

1. Describe some of the bonding behaviors between a mother and her baby?

2. What is the basis of building a relationship according to John Bowlby?

3. List five signs of RAD?

4. As a parent, or trainer of children, what is your first objective in training them?

5. Explain how building boundaries and limits builds trust?

6. How would a set schedule help a child become a "believer"?

7. Why does a child identify having their physical needs met with being loved?

8. In building relationships, how important are routine family activities.

9. Explain how a parent and a child become "bonded" and capable of facing life's challenges based on food, sleep, exercise and chores?

10. Is it healthy for a child to act so as to attract discipline in order to bond?

Chapter Two:

‑‑⚜‑‑

ACCEPTABLE:
Standards of Conduct

PARENTING SUPERVISION PRINCIPLES

4   *Effective parenting begins with the clarification and definition of your basic goals, values, core character traits, you desire for your children.*

5   *Parenting supervisors must communicate and model the desired core values.*

6   *Children must clearly understand the values they are expected to maintain.*

7   *Respect for parenting authority is essential in forming character in children.*

In his famous "I have a Dream" speech, Martin Luther King, Jr. said he dreamed of the day when all Americans "will be judged not by the color of their skin but by the *content of their charac*ter".

Think of "character" as an empty cup. Each child is created by God with the "cup", an inherited framework that will later contain values, rules, standards, and boundaries to determine "right" from "wrong". The ingredients of the "cup" are the values, the congruent behaviors, and the corrective discipline that begin in the early life of the child. This internal mechanism comes "by nature", but is filled, or trained by "nurture". The end result at some later date is what we call "good character." This is the bundle of beliefs by which individuals guide their lives for as long as they live their lives on the earth.

Tony Dungy, renowned coach of the Baltimore Colts and the Tampa Bay Buccaneers, noted the importance of "good character" even in professional sports. Talent scouts often labeled a prospect with "DNDC – *Do Not Draft because of Character!" (Uncommon*, p.4). Everything a person does, including his ability to play football, is tempered by the quality of that person's character. Who he or she *is* by nature *and* by nurture!

Any parenting series purporting to instruct parents on "how to raise kids" must begin with core values, basic beliefs, (the "content of character") the virtues of character, the intrinsic *good* that has first claim on our consciences to know and do *right* instead of *wrong*! These are our basic beliefs about what is important. Those beliefs will guide our responses to everything that happens to us in life.

The "cup of character" is, a) Collectively, our core values which represent a set of community values (usually parental values) that translate into rules, boundaries, and laws, *basic beliefs* ...objective reference points for evaluating individual behaviors!   b) how well a child is able to live his or her life by making good decisions under supervision and corrective discipline!

Character is the *end product* of this *information-in-practice* process.   It is the built-in mechanism, framework, guidance-device, (or whatever you want to call it!) that allows a person to be independent. Basic character is what makes it possible to live *successfully by the rules* in the real world. How can that happen?

THE GOAL: A CHRISTIAN CHARACTER

First, as parenting supervisors you must have a clear vision of the values you desire in your children. These values must be visualized so that they can be simply communicated to the child. Both the supervisor and the child must understand that violations of the path leading to these values must be disciplined.

CORE VALUES

Thus, we begin this "character-building" training with values, morals, life goals, aspirations! For purposes of this training manual the "Christian values" commonly accepted in America will be the basis of our ideal "Character". These values form the core of our character. If you know what you want your child *to be*, that child is more likely to be it. Your morals are your actions measured by your ethics. A person is a "moral" person when he or she "acts" with integrity according to his or her inner core values, or standards. This integrity produces a genuine, sincere person whose choices of conduct are mostly "right choices" according to that person's character. Two early thinker put it like this,

Moral philosophy is *hard thought* about *right action.* - Socrates

Morality is not a subject; it is *a life put to the test* in dozens of moments. -Paul Tillich

The bar has been set high by the writer of Proverbs (22:6) for Christian parents in training their children. Note the three translations below:

Train up a child in the way he should go,
And when he is old he will not depart from it. (New
King James Version)

Teach your children to choose the right path, and when
they are older, they will remain upon it. (New Living
Translation)

Teach your children right from wrong, and when they
are grown they will still do right. (Contemporary
Translation)

So, it is important to carefully consider your core
values for several reasons:

1) Your core values help *guide you towards your*
   goals, rather than your life being controlled by
   self-serving motives, customs, accidental
   occurrences, bad habits, impulses, or emotions.
   You must have a clear vision of where you are
   going before you can ever get there.

2) Values and morals serve like a "pep rally" *to*
   inspire and motivate you, giving you energy and a
   zest for living your life. Depressed people have
   often lost sight of their missions and goals for
   living.

3) Your values are the elements in "your anchor"
   that *stabilize you* in the storms of life.
   Sometimes only your "commitment" to a value or
   goal holds you on course during stormy times.
   One internet saying is, *"Life isn't about how to*
   survive the storm, but how to dance in the rain!

4) Sensitivity to a failure to live up to your basic
   values may lead to unproductive guilt; but a
   comparative analysis of your actions and values
   provides the means for life improvements. You
   can't *do* better if you do not *know* better!

5) High values and some history of success meeting those goals are necessary for *healthy self-image*. This defines our need to honestly see ourselves as others see us.

6) (Verbally) Claimed values that are not exercised in behaviors result in hypocrisy and phony sham. Basic honesty is demanded *to recognize the difference in pretended values and actual conduct*.

When a person's actions, or conduct choices, are congruent with that person's core values we usually describe him or her as *"a very genuine, sincere person"*. We might disagree with their core values, but we respect them for living according to them! Conversely, we do not respect a person who says one thing and does something else.

The goal of effective supervision (or, training) of children is:

1) *To instill the core values, basic beliefs; then*
2) *To monitor the applications of the "values" to his or her life behaviors, and*
3) *To correct (or, discipline) the child's behaviors that are incongruent with the instilled values; and*
4) *To produce a person of character living a moral ethical lifestyle.*

Such parental supervision produces healthy adults with character. In addition, the adult with character has a much better chance of thriving in a hostile world. A person's morals matter!

MORAL LIVING

What do we mean by the expression: "moral living?" It is one thing to decide on a set of core values, it is something else to bring those values into the actual conduct of a child. "Moral living" defines how closely a person is living by that person's own standards, or core values!

The Palmist helps us understand this process. READ: Psalms 51:2-14.

First, it is the *emotional development* to feel guilty when we violate our values:

> *Wash me thoroughly from my iniquity*
> *And cleanse me from my sin.*
> *3 For I know my transgressions,*
> *And my sin is ever before me.*

Second, we must *be socially attached* so we will accept our responsibility for behaving in the agreed upon ways towards our group:

> *Against You, You only, I have sinned and done what is evil in Your sight,*

Finally, with our *cognitive abilities* we are able to place ourselves in another person's shoes with empathy for the group:

> *Restore to me the joy of Your Salvation and sustain me with a willing spirit. Then I will teach transgressors Your ways, and sinners will be converted to You.*

Essentially, the development of moral character equips a person with a conduct (behaviors) goal, or mission, that helps that person know where he or she wants to go, and what they will look like when they get there!

Steven Covey (1992), the author of *The Seven Habits of Highly Effective People*, said it like this:

> *"Many people set goals and strive for years to achieve one after another, only to discover when they get to the*

end goals that they didn't want to go there." He says, "no one on their death bed ever complains that they should have spent more time in the office."

In another book, *First Things First,* Covey (1994) says everyone and every family (and every organization, every nation, etc.) should have a well thought out "Mission Statement," a set of values, or a guiding philosophy of life.

Effective parenting begins with the clarification and definition of these basic goals, values, core character traits you desire for your children.

However, a parenting "mission statement" must begin with self-evaluation! Parents must ask themselves intimate questions about themselves. These questions do a self-study of our most basic beliefs and core values. It is very improbable that a child will *become* something that a parent *is not.* Self-examination identifies and defines the core values of the parents, or child care supervisors. The visible, demonstrated "lived-out" values that a child sees in the supervisor will more than likely become their values.

PARENTAL CORE VALUES?

What should these "core values" be in your parenting? Any answer to this question depends on the background, training, and experiences of the persons asking the question. However, from a Christian perspective the values must come from the lofty standards of the Bible. The Acceptable Behaviors Choices System is based on the Judeo-Christian traditions revealed in the Bible and prevalent in most of America today. In the closing pages of this book the ultimate standard is set for those of us who espouse the Christian values.

It is sometimes useful to reduce these major values to key words, or phrases. These "tags" or target goals become the public "tip of the ice-berg" in our values system. A long growing list of behaviors, or conduct experiences will be developed under each of these "targets" of measurement as a child grows and develops.

Several "lists" could be compiled that describe the content of our character, or our core values. Tom Lichona, of the Center for the 4th and 5th R (Respect and Responsibility) suggests a workable list of ten "values":

- *Wisdom*, or good judgment
- *Justice*, or respect for rights of others
- *Fortitude*, ability to do right in face of difficulty
- *Self-Control*, ability to govern ourselves
- *Positive Attitude*, an asset to everyone
- *Hard work*, just doing it
- *Integrity*, standing up for what you believe
- *Gratitude*, counting our blessings
- *Humility*, the foundation of the whole moral life

The Georgia Department of Education lists three major character values that should be taught in the public schools of Georgia. They are:

- Good Citizenship
- Respect for Others
- Respect for self

At Raintree Village Children's Home, we have ten "Core Values" that we set as conduct goals for the children in our care. These are based on the Judeo-Christian values of America. They are defined in terms of the Scriptures as applied to the standards in most American communities. The following guide named the "Pillars of Character" define what is *acceptable* at Raintree Village:

- Respect
- Responsibility
- Fairness
- Competence

- Trustworthiness
- Citizenship
- Caring
- Belonging
- Serving
- Spirituality

Other organizations might have a different set of values. However, the core values held by any group tend to mold the mission statement of that organization. Our behaviors, or conduct, tend to follow the lofty goals or core values we esteem to be venerable, or highly respected.

Begin by picturing what you want your child *to be* in terms of key words, or target-tags that suggest many different behaviors. For example, if one of your targets is "Respect", you must then visualize what your child would *look like, or be* if this target was met... at 3 years old! Or at 16 years old! Whenever!

What are some key values, target-words, you want for your children? For now, just list the key words!

QUESTIONNAIRE #1:

Desired "Core Values" For Your Children
- List your "target" core values below as "key words".
- Rate (overall, generally) how successful you believe you are in instilling these in your children. ("1" = not successful; "10" = very successful)

    1) _____

    2) _____

    3) _____

    4) _____

    5) _____

    6) _____

    7) _____

    8) _____

    9) _____

    10)_____

11)_____

12)_____

Now, think about what you, the parents or child care trainers, consider important "values" for your lives. Use the following questionnaire to list your actual "core values": *What are some important core values you possess?*

QUESTIONNAIRE #2:

Parent's Current Core Values

- What are your values now? Name your values, virtues using one word for each value.
- Rate yourself, (using a scale of "1" to "10" with "1" = not much and "10" = very much) on how much influence your core values are evidenced in your conduct.

1) _____
2) _____
3) _____
4) _____
5) _____
6) _____
7) _____
8) _____
9) _____
10) _____
11) _____
12) _____

Look over the two lists. Especially notice that you may be expecting to instill some values in a child that you do not possess. It is important to see "how well you are doing".

Compare the two lists you have made. Are the two lists similar? Different? Why? This comparison will help child care supervisors understand how well they are modeling the core values they want for their children.

A CODE OF ETHICS

Next, ask yourself what is your "Code of Ethics", and how well are you living up to it? This exercise helps you put a number of "values" together with some expected "behaviors".

A business, or profession, may approach the matter of "values" and "core character" under their Code of Ethics. "Ethics" are the rules or standards governing the conduct of a person or the members of a profession, such as *medical ethics.*

Ethics involves the study and application of "right" conduct. Persons who ask, "What ought I to do" are likely to be asking an ethical question. They are concerned that their actions are right or wrong based on their values and standards. Some baseline of "right" must be established and recognized before violations of ethics can be identified.

CHARACTER TRANSFORMATION

Second, whether or not the appropriate character will develop in the child will depend on the effectiveness of two processes of your supervision:

1. How effective the supervisor establishes the *use of their parental power, or authority.*

2. How effective the supervisors (parents, guardians, significant others) are in *communicating the desired values to the child.*

These two interaction processes permeate the relations between children and their parents in all typical family living situations. This includes such regular interaction times as family meals and the routine communications of family life such as getting ready for school, getting ready for bed, etc.

The processes are vividly present in the face-to-face corrective interactions between a parent and child when discipline is required. Several characteristics of the interactive process are significant in framing the result: tone of voice, consistency of practice, clarity of communications, etc.

LIVING WITH AUTHORITY

On a casual visit to any new recruit training base one is impressed with the barking orders from the drill sergeant and the redundant ...MARCHING...MARCHING...MARCHING............ for countless hours on the parade field!

The casual visitor may ask:

"Why do they march so much?"

"What good does it do to "stay in step", or go "right face"?

"What does this marching have to do with fighting a war!?"

The field commander explains: *"The officer of the day has the authority to command obedience. The recruits learn to obey the marching orders (Right face, Forward, March, Halt, etc.!")* for one reason: SO THE RECRUIT CAN LEARN TO OBEY THE OFFICER IN AUTHORITY! In the time of battle, the ability to simply obey instructions may be life-saving!

PARENTING POWER

By definition, the exercise of "authority" is the "lawful right" to enforce obedience. Jesus, the master teacher, taught "as one with authority" (Matthew 7:29). Near the end of creation, God granted man the "authority over the fish of the sea, over the birds of the air, and over every creeping thing on the earth" (Genesis 1:26). Government has been vested, gifted, with authority from God (Romans 13).

Our world is one in which we continually find ourselves under "some" authority as a citizen, employee, student, church-member, or soldier. Other more routine relationships of authority include the husband/wife roles and the larger men/women roles. We must learn to live with authority. Neither "authority" nor "obedience" is a bad word! These words define the relationship between parents and their children.

AUTHORITY AS A GIFT!

Authority is GIVEN...it's a gift! (Mark 11:27-33). There are basic responsibilities that go with the gift of authority. In fact, when the gift of authority is conveyed, those who resist it, or violate it, actually resist God! (Romans 13:2). The person (governor, husband, king, church leader, parent, supervisor), for whatever reason, is placed "in charge"!

Another way to understand authority is to see it as *"vested trust"* due to experience and wisdom. Those who have had the experiences, demonstrated expertise, developed the wisdom, *and survived* with linking successes are vested by others with trust. We tend to comply with the authorities of experience, wisdom, and achievement.

A military general stands before his troops! His personal confidence calls for obedience to his barked-out commands. Across his vested uniform, over his heart, are his ribbons of experience. Each ribbon certifies the battles he has survived and the victories he has won. The new recruits easily see him as one who knows what going to battle is all about! They learn to trust him, but the initial obedience is solely a matter of obedience to his vested authority.

PARENTING POWER (AUTHORITY EXERCISED)

Basic authority then is nothing more than power that is granted (gifted) to someone to enforce obedience. Authority is the "right to rule". In this sense, parents are vested with the "power to rule" in their interactions with their children. Parents have a *strategic* (powerful, important) influence in the lives of their children simply because they are "the parents"! The parenting position is vested by God, and society in most cases, with basic authority to rule.

Children, obey your parents in the Lord, for this is right. Honor your father and mother, for this is the first commandment with promise that you may live long on the earth. (Ephesians 6:1).

By its very nature, the exercise of any authority is usually met initially with resistance by those who are being "ruled". Such is often true in the interactions between parents and children as the children grow and develop toward their adult independence.

Thus, parents are gifted by God (and our world) with the right to rule children! It is their responsibility to supervise their children. The result of their parenting will only be as effective as their quality use of authority. They have a delegated authority to instill character, mettle, core values in children. The interactions between the supervisors and the supervisees may become strained, antagonistic, and even rebellious in the character-building process! However, the importance of developing good parenting skills is mirrored in the possible bad outcomes of the children...including the fact that they may "not live long on the earth"! Too much is at stake for parents to misuse the trust invested in them by God.

COMMUNICATING CORE VALUES

The second task, or process, that must be effectively managed by parenting supervisors is in *communicating (and instilling) in their children the desired values, or virtues, each child needs* for healthy independent maturity in the real world.

Train up a child in the way he should go: and when he is old, he will not depart from it. (KJV)

This task involves the process of "training" a child with the essential "values" that will last a lifetime! How do we do this?! The very concept of "the way he *should* go" creates in every sincere parent both a dreaded fear of failure and an apprehensive desire to DO IT RIGHT! Two things are involved in this training process:

1) Training that will be "right" by some standard of right and wrong, and

2) Training that will "last for a lifetime" - sort of like giving the child a built-in *moral* GPS system for the rest of his/her life!

In the previous sections the importance of a "mission statement" for your parenting role was defined in terms of your core values. You were asked to define and evaluate your own basic values. These form your basic foundation in being an effective parenting supervisor. It is critically important for you to remember, review, and rehearse your "core values" on a daily basis.

Parents, we learned, have vested power to rule in the lives of their children. Our parent-power is due to this vested authority, but it is effective only when the power is used to effectively communicate values and basic virtues to our children. The remainder of this section suggests three ways this can be done.

POWER OF A GOOD EXAMPLE

First, you become effective in communicating your "mission statement" by your influential *presence*, your persona-authority. Psychologists call it "modeling".

Christians call it being a "good example" or, just letting your light shine!

These things command and teach. Let no one despise your youth, but be an example to the believers in word, in conduct, in love, in spirit, F6 in faith, in purity. Till I come, give attention to reading, to exhortation, to doctrine. (1 Timothy 4:11)

This text provides a good outline for setting a good example for our children:

In word

This would include the things we say, and the way we say them! Talking is the basic mode of communicating with our children.   However, it might include writing notes, posting posters, or even listening to music!

In conduct

Conduct is the manner in which we act, or control ourselves! Our conduct is our demeanor; the way we behave toward others. A good "conductor" is a medium of transmission much like metal conducts heat! Our conduct is really the way we act, particularly in relation to our ethics and values.

In love

Love is that deep, tender, ineffable feeling of affection and solicitude toward a person, such as that arising from kinship, recognition of attractive qualities, or a sense of underlying oneness.

The Bible defines love like this:

Love is patient, love is kind, and is not jealous; love does not brag and is not arrogant, does not act unbecomingly; it does not seek its own, is not provoked, does not take into account a wrong suffered, does not rejoice in unrighteousness, but rejoices with the truth; bears all things, believes all things, hopes all things, endures all things. Love never fails. (1 Corinthians 13:4-8 *NAS)*

Love" conjures up all kinds of ideas and associations ranging from a deep feeling of attachment and desire to simply providing for the wants and needs of another. Over time, this attachment deepens and becomes more complex as the parent attends to the increasing dependency needs that require not only physical care and nurturing, but also daily guidance, attention, and at times, play and entertainment during those early years. In fact, dependency remains a basic need for much of childhood and into adolescence until children begin to form their own identities.

Love is the capacity to provide for these basic dependency needs while allowing for the development of a strong, positive attachment that is based on the parents' ability to meet both the child's emotional and physical needs.

Paul continues his instructions to Timothy (1 Timothy 4:11) in how to communicate his example:

In spirit

Perhaps this could be better understood by being an example "in emotions!" Our emotional reactions to our children, and how we express our emotions, speak volumes about whether or not we are "mad, sad, glad, or even guilty!"

In faith

We will take this to mean: LET YOUR RELIGION SHOW! Your children ought to know what you believe by seeing you in action! "I'd rather see a sermon, than hear one any day!"

In purity

Purity has to do with sincerity, genuineness! You being the REAL THING! Children can spot "a phony" a mile away! Sincerity is generally understood to be truth in word and act. One who means what he says is a sincere person. One who does not mean what he says is not a sincere man, and is perhaps even a hypocrite. Because of its purity the term sincerity has endeared itself to us. We love sincere people. We also love to be known as sincere people. But there is a deeper reference, and that is the inner being, the soul.

> *Sincerity means to act according to the dictates of the inner self, to obey the inner divine "Will of God" enthroned on our conscience!*

Thus, the personal example of a parenting supervisor is his or her strongest promotion of personal authority. We literally set ourselves forward to be followed. The message the children receive and follow depends on how they perceive the model set before them.

PARENTING COMMUNICATIONS

Second, our values must be communicated by our interactions with the children! By definition, parent/child communications mean *every interaction process* (verbal, non-verbal, virtual- and meta-communications!) as the means of communication. The content of the communications process is our "oughts" and "ought-nots" of our value system.

Paraphrasing the words of Proverbs: "train the child where to go"! The parent must decide this! It cannot be left to the inexperienced, and untried, child! Nor can parents turn it over to others, regardless of who they are or what they might know.

NEGATIVE COMMUNICATIONS

As a child grows, love demands that limits and boundaries be established. Setting limits is the parental process of communicating the danger-markings of life, much like the flashing signals define the roadbed in construction zones.

Why are limits (boundaries) so important?

A. Limits teach our children *how to function in the world.* If parents don't set limits early in life, life will set those limits in a big way, often resulting in suffering that could have been avoided.

B. Limit-setting helps the development of self-discipline and *the formation of a conscience* in a child. Consistent limits for a child help him/her internalize the parents' strengths. The child begins to form a sense of safety in the world. This "sense of safety" comes from the child's ability to control themselves, their impulses, and to direct their energies into good productive achievements.

C. Setting limits is an act of love. It *prepares your child for adult life.* Living in a social world requires daily consideration of each other's rights and desires. Recognizing and respecting the boundaries of others is love in practice.

So, the negative limits of saying "No" produces positive results in the parent/child relationship. Establishing and defining "boundaries" for children will not only provide safety for the young, but direction for when they are older. All of their lives they will be restricted, limited, by the boundaries of laws, possibilities, gender, position, and time.

However, positive communications are even more valuable in the parent/child interactions.

INFORMATION EXPLOSION

A cultural development that has significantly impacted the family is the explosion of mass media and mass communication, particularly the internet and social networking. Television and internet technology have changed the information/communication environment within which parents are trying to monitor and control the development of their children. The massive exposure to all kinds of information, and particularly information that is unhealthy or beyond the scope of a child's developmental age, has placed parents in the untenable position of battling outside influences that tear at the parent-child relationship. This modern module of information can be a threat or a boom to parenting. It depends on the authoritative management of the supervisors.

Parenting supervisors must compete with many other voices in transmitting their values to their children. However, parents in many ways are also in a very favorable position to have the greatest influence due to time, attachment, and motivation.

Nevertheless, the strength of the parent-child relationship is more important than ever. It is our primary means of keeping our children safe, helping them to navigate the world, and assisting them to develop personal strengths for making the right choices.

FORMATION OF COALITIONS

A third tool for instilling our core values in our children is to form valuable coalitions with good people. In addition to basic communications *within* the family to enhance or expand our abilities to build values in a child, parents should enlist help *from outside* the family, alliances with others for help.

A coalition is formed when others are brought together for strength toward some goal. Parents form coalitions with coaches, teachers, peers of the child, and even non-human things like dogs or cars, to influence the conduct and behavior of a child.

"Who's in charge?" is sometimes like the key-stone-cop joke about "Who's on third!?" Everything gets very confusing and dangerous when parents lose power over the behaviors of their children. Sometimes the balance of power is shifted in the safe, right direction when others are brought into alliance with the parent's desires and plans. Effective parents realize that sometimes the coach of the team, or good friends at school, or some other outside person or group has more influence over their child than they do. However, the parent must still exercise their "parent-power" to manage these alliances. Why would a parent endorse, or even allow, a close coalition of their child with a person or group that has major different "core values"? Parents must use others outside the family as a natural result of living in the world at large. However, they can exercise some control over both which groups to have contact with and the amount of time spent.

The essential point is this: To help our children develop these two things, 1) An *internal right and wrong standard of conduct,* and 2) An *ability to act according to that standard.*

In Summary, the initial role of parents is to train their children to be safe by developing internal controls for behavior! They do this by teaching them to be submissive in obedience to the legitimate authorities in their world. However, the long term goal of parenting is for the child to become independent, self-directing as a productive adult living by the values of their community.

Discussion Questions:

   1. What is your definition of "character"?

2. What part do you think "core values" play in our "character"?

3. Explain how our core values can lead us to our goals in life.

4. Discuss how our values can dictate what occupation, or work we are in.

5. Discuss whether or not it is "fair" to expect your children to have your values?

6. Name the two interaction processes that determine the formation of character in our children?

7. Discuss why "teaching obedience" to our children is so important?

8. Discuss how "authority" is a gift?

9. What is the single most important element in effectively communicating values to our children?

10. Define "communication" in the "parent/child" relationship?

11. How do "Coalition formations" help us transmit values to our children? Name a few?

Chapter Three

⚜

BEHAVIORS:
Defining Right Conduct

PARENTING SUPERVISION PRINCIPLES

8 *Healthy families produce healthy children.*

9 *Children develop the inner strength of character by submitting to the daily routines of personal care, social interactions, and duties in a healthy family.*

10 *Build trust...teach a child to believe.*

11 *Children learn to respect personal boundaries and community rules by living in healthy families.*

What does a "healthy family" look like? What makes an "unhealthy family" different? How can you identify the traits in your family that would define it as "healthy"? What symptoms will be evident in a family system that make it sick, or "unhealthy"? Parenting supervisors must develop a clear vision of the two extreme boundaries that distinguish "healthy" families from "unhealthy" families. These boundaries are defined in terms of how the parents and children interact, their verbal and non-verbal communications.

In this section parenting supervisors will learn to define the goal values, or core character traits, in terms of smaller bits of behavior in the daily lives of the family. The purpose, or mission of a healthy family is to *live the values* of the family. The process for accomplishing this mission is *how effectively a family establishes a healthy structure* which includes boundaries, rules and choices. The following chapters explore these issues.

CREATING A HEALTHY FAMILY

A professional child care "family" such as Raintree Village Children's Home is NOT a typical, natural family! We are not "mom-dad-and-the kids"! First, our "families" include children from many different family units. Secondly, our "children" come from many places and from many different family life backgrounds. We are *not* a "typical family". However, like a social lab, child care group homes provide a good backdrop to study "healthy" families. Many of the issues typical to dysfunctional families can be seen clearly in this setting.

Therefore, it is worthwhile for us to understand what a typical, natural, "healthy" family is about by contrasting it with children from "unhealthy" families! What traits set healthy families apart from those that are unhealthy? Needless to say, many of the children in a professional child setting were placed in care from very dysfunctional, unhealthy families! Most of them experience daily problems related to their earlier years of training in dysfunctional homes.

WHAT IS A "HEALTHY FAMILY"?

There are certain characteristics that stand out in families that seem to be successful in providing a safe, growing environment for children. These homes are "safe havens" for children, where love, trust, and mutual aid abound. Healthy families are not perfect! Misunderstandings, with bickering and arguing are there, but not all the time. When there is conflict, or resistance, the family has a healthy way of restoring peace.

Like any family, there will be challenges...such as sickness, personal problems, traumatic episodes, and family crises that threaten the peace and security of that family. This is normal. However, the healthy family system is maintained with definable traits:

Consistent leadership:

Parents can be counted on to provide care for their children. The key words are "can be counted on"! The parental roles as providers were easily identified by the children. They understood who was in charge.

Healthy Relationships:

Children are consistently treated with respect, and do not fear emotional, verbal, physical, or sexual abuse. Treated with respect! These children feel accepted and safe. A major defining trait of healthy families is the sense of safety.

Organized:

Children are given responsibilities appropriate to their age and are not expected to take on parental responsibilities. In healthy families the family roles are clearly marked and faithfully performed. There is order and not chaos! Everyone understands that certain things must be done...clean the house, prepare meals, transports, etc. Tasks are assigned and performed with loyalty.

Clear Expectations:

Rules are explicit and remain consistent, but with flexibility. The children understand what is expected of them, but they also know that the parents may often "cut some slack" because of the family love relationship. The family is neither a confined prison nor a free-love lovefest! The rules are fewer than more but submission to the rules is expected. Rules of the parenting supervisors are clearly defined and carefully communicated. Not only must the child know them, but they must be submissive to them.

Respected Boundaries:

Personal and family boundaries are clearly identified and maintained with individual functioning roles. The children are allowed to be "children". They do not function as "parents". Boundaries of respect protect the responsibilities and the duties of each family role.

Peaceful:

Family "expectations" and individual "performances" are balanced resulting in a peaceful, satisfying family unit. In a healthy family the ebb and flow of daily routines and family conflicts smoothly evolve into a stronger bond between the family members.

Ideally, children grow up in families where they learn to feel worthwhile and valuable. Children growing up in such supportive environments are likely to form healthy relationships in adulthood.

All healthy families, whatever the makeup, are about love and care and watching out for each other. Healthy families are not perfect; they may have yelling, bickering, misunderstanding, tension, hurt, and anger - but in the end the family is stabilized by the love that binds them together.

In summary, healthy families are places where emotional expression is allowed and accepted. Family members can freely ask for and give attention. Rules tend to be made explicit and remain consistent, but with some flexibility to adapt to individual needs and particular situations. Healthy families allow for individuality; each member is encouraged to pursue his or her own interests, and boundaries between individuals are honored and respected. Children in healthy families are consistently treated with respect, and do not fear emotional, verbal, physical, or sexual abuse. Parents can be counted on to provide care for their children. Children are given responsibilities appropriate to their age and are not expected to take on parental responsibilities. Finally, in healthy families everyone makes mistakes; mistakes are allowed. Perfection is unattainable, unrealistic, and potentially dull and sterile. Most importantly, children feel safe in healthy families.

WHAT IS AN "UNHEALTHY FAMILY"?

However, families may fail to provide for many of their children's emotional and physical needs. These children may spend years in a "dysfunctional" home where daily communications are emotionally draining and low self-esteem is common. Children from these dysfunctional families:

1. May be forced to take sides in conflicts between parents.

2. Experience "reality shifting" in which what is said contradicts what is actually happening (e.g., "black becomes white", and "good becomes bad" when what a parent says contradicts what a child observes).

3. Be ignored, discounted, or criticized for their feelings, thoughts, and behaviors.

4. Their parents are inappropriately intrusive, overly involved and protective, or,

5. The parents are inappropriately distant and uninvolved with their children.

6. Have excessive structure and demands placed on their time, choice of friends, or behavior; or conversely, receive no guidelines or structure.

7. Experience rejection or preferential treatment.

8. These children do not have full and direct communication with other family members, either the nuclear family or the extended family.

9. They may even be influenced, allowed or encouraged to use drugs or alcohol. Many children learn how to drink "in the home".

10. They are locked out of the house, both emotionally and sometimes actually!

11. Abuse is often present as these children are slapped, hit, scratched, punched, kicked, or "thumped" or worse!

WHAT IS "MISSING" IN THE UNHEALTHY FAMILY?

Trust! Basic human faith, or personal trust, is what is often missing in a typical placement of a child in a professional child care facility. Years of abuse and neglect of the child in a dysfunctional family results in the loss of trust in the world, others, and even themselves. They do not trust the words of others, particularly the "big people" –adults! They have failed so often that they do not trust their own behaviors and actions. These children have lost their sense of self-worth. The loss of trust has locked these children into a losing mode in school, in personal relationships, and in developing their own personal identities.

Faith-based parenting supervisors may have an advantage over community-based approaches *because of* their focus on the importance of faith. Doubt destroys, but basic faith and trust build confidence and personal inward strength. Arguably, children have an innate need to believe.

Thus, *the basic responsibility of parenting supervisors,* is to build trust between the child and the supervisor. A supervisor of children is duty-bound to be truthful, fair, and trustworthy! Children, and their supervisors, interact and communicate in either a positive or negative way. Supervisors must set the example, but the child must learn to be submissive in the day-to-day behaviors of life. It is in these daily behaviors where trust is eventually established and grows.

BASIC BEHAVIORS THAT BUILD TRUST

Trust begins the day a child is born and begins to interact with the "big people"! The learning process continues as the child care supervisors and the child mutually interact in all the physical and environmental situations of daily life. In the early years it is more as a care-giver and a child, but the relationship gradually changes over the years to a child care "*supervisor*" and a young person moving toward independence from outside supervision.

An illustration of how "authority" relates during the early years might be this:

A mother sits across from a child on the floor and says "Roll the ball to me," and the child learns the joy of "rolling the ball!"

Actually, the parent has taken a commanding position, with authority, and given a specific clearly communicated authoritative directive. The dependent child is the recipient of something that brings joy, satisfaction. Repetitions of this care-giver/child interaction results in satisfactory compliance by the child. It is a learned self-help process with authoritative *oversight! This is parenting supervision.*

43

Thus, specific behaviors must be defined as the garden to grow the desired traits of character in a child. The normal daily acts of living (eating, sleeping, working, etc.) are usually the most fertile fields for teaching submission. The goal, however, is to train the child for life!

CHANGE FACTORS

The negative effect of change on a child varies. Often when a child has been placed in a child care facility due to the bad things that can happen in their natural families (e. i. divorce, incarceration, abuse or neglect) the child usually goes through predictable negative behavior changes. The stress they feel, or depression, may result in the display of strong emotions such as anger, sadness, confusion, grief, guilt, shame, and anxiety!

Each child is different. Each one will react to the trauma in his or her life, however, according to predictable differences. These differences must be considered to properly train a child's character.

Age

Younger children may be hyperactive when they are actually depressed, while older children may become melancholy or withdrawn. Young children may regress to earlier behaviors such as bed-wetting, or thumb sucking. School-age children may begin to fail in school, or complain about frequent headaches or stomachaches. Teens are most likely to just act out! A teenager may show overt anger, or resentment, or outright rudeness. Romantic relationships are often used by teens to "escape" their pain.

Gender

Boys are more likely than girls to show strong emotional reactions to life situations. Girls, on the other hand, may be hurting just as much but they tend to "hold it in", hide their true feelings, and internalize the conflict they feel.

Temperament

Children get their "temperament" from nature and nurturing. The easy-going child will usually do what is expected of them more often than the strong-willed reactive child. The reactive child is usually disruptive of daily routines. The easy-going child finds the routines supportive and comforting.

Living situation

The child's room, living situation, is both one of the most powerful means of changing the child and one of the worst deterrents to change! The child is forced to adjust to a new bed, a new room, a new house, a new school, a new "family"!

All of these differences, and others not listed, may be used by the parents and other child care supervisors to train the child. Parents use their power (authority gifted as parents) to manipulate the differences to work toward the goals for the child's behavior. The parent is in charge of the components that bring about change in the child.

However, the differences especially demonstrate that "one size fits all" just will not work in training our children. Each of the children in a family has to be treated *differently*, but at the same time...*the same!* That's our challenge, to be fair but effective!

THE STRONGEST FORCE FOR CHANGE!

The child in your care has many issues to face, not the least of which is "YOU"! *You, the adult parenting supervisor, is the strongest single factor for change in the child's life!* In fact, during the early formative years YOU are the MOST IMPORTANT single person in your child's life! You are the strongest regulator for change in your child!

Your example, or modeling, the expectations of the family values

Your emotional disposition, particularly in the heat of battle, when things get tough!

Your actions, and reactions, to highly stressful situations and behaviors,

Your ability to stay balanced in the multifaceted tasks of supervising changing, developing children,

Your management of time to keep from becoming absorbed by the increasing demands of daily living and emotional struggles,

Your fair and equitable development of personal relationships with all the members of your family.

HELPING CHILDREN COPE WITH CHANGE

Talk

Be honest and straightforward about how living in "your house" will affect the child's life. Talk to the child on his or her level about their feelings and your responsibilities.

Encourage

This word means to take some of your "courage" and give it to them! Let your children know that you have an open door policy for each one of them! Be sure they know they can ask you questions and get answers about almost anything.

Reassure

Children under care are often confused and frightened by their surroundings. Their worlds seem turned upside down. You need to let them know that "It will be O.K.!" Don't make promises that you cannot keep, but do reassure your children of the future.

Explain

Keep your children advised on changes that may take place in the home. Explain the reasons why the changes were being made.

Kids are Kids

Be sure you react to each child in an age appropriate way. Let each one grieve, or celebrate, appropriately.

Rules

The ABC system is based on rules, but the major focus is on "choices". Help your children understand how important it is to the entire family, when one member acts in a negative way. Rules define what is "right" and "wrong". Rules provide boundaries for a child to gain a sense of independence, confidence and to feel safe.

Respect

Children benefit when they witness positive relations with others around them. Be respectful of each child, those in authority, and others in the home. Do not ever ask a child to "take sides"! Be respectful of their feelings.

Trust

Again...our job as parenting supervisors is to equip a child with the tools for learning how to trust! Trust is assured resting of the mind on the integrity, veracity, justice, friendship, or other sound principle, of another person; confidence; reliance.

BEHAVIORS AND BOUNDARIES

What is a boundary? It is a line that marks the limits of an area; a dividing line. The Webster dictionary definition is:

- Something (such as a river, a fence, or an imaginary line) that shows where an area ends and another area begins

- A point or limit that indicates where two things become different

- Unofficial rules about what should not be done: limits that define acceptable behavior

What are some examples of "boundaries"? City limits, fences, walls, ditches, "(Your rights end at the other person's nose!)" What does *that* mean? It may mean the difference in a physical assault and possible jail time, and freedom to be friends. Boundaries may be social, or psychological. What are some other "boundaries"? Think about it.

QUID PRO QUO!

"In the sweat of thy brow shalt thou eat bread" (Gen. 3:19). One of the very important consequences of this judgment that our Almighty God pronounced on all human beings is the principle of *quid pro quo*. We get nothing for nothing. Everything we want or need, we must earn. People usually only treasure possessions that they have earned or paid for.

A Biblical example of this is found in 1st Samuel chapter 2. In the relationship of Hannah and Eli a child was desired. Hannah prayed for a child, and she got what she prayed for! What did it cost her? Good children do not come cheap!

In Deuteronomy 5:16 children are told of the rich blessings from learning to obey parents, *"as the LORD thy God hath commanded thee; that thy days may be prolonged, and that it may go well with thee, in the land which the LORD thy God giveth thee."*

The child will have a good life on condition that he honors — that is, obeys, submits to — his father and his mother. This promise of "prolonged days" is repeated in Ephesians 6:1. The passport to a good, long life is to learn the importance of submission. Learning submission is not a weakness, but a strength! Rather than making a child dependent, it teaches him or her how to be independent.

In 1st Samuel 3:4-8 an example of a child's submission is given: When Samuel heard his name called in the dark of night, he immediately got up, ran to Eli and said, *"Here I am, you called me."* But Eli told him that he had not called, and instructed him to go back and lie down, which he did. When Samuel again heard his name being called, he again immediately got up — although he had just been told that Eli had not called him — went to Eli again and said, *"Here I am, you called me."* For a second time he was assured that Eli had not called him and instructed to return to bed, which he did. For a third time he heard his name being called and, although twice he had been told that Eli had not called him, he nevertheless got up immediately, went to Eli and said, *"Here I am, you called me."*

SUPERVISING A CHILD'S BEHAVIORS: *Obedience*

Thus far we have noted that two of the most important roles a parenting supervisor performs are:

a) *Instructing a child on what is "right", and*

b). *Modeling a good example.*

We have noted the importance of core values as the goals we seek to instill in each child. Helping the child *experience* these values and adopt them for his or her own <u>is</u> the task we must accomplish. The variables of this task include the [1]*age* and [2]*gender* of the child, [3]*abilities* of the child and [4]*time*. The process may be defined in terms of the child's "behaviors", the individual actions of everyday life.

Next, we focused on the parenting supervisors' ability to model the values before the child. Those who supervise the conduct of children must be able to *see* (or, visualize!) the finished product! What a child with character will look like! For this to be accomplished what is "right" (according to the accepted values) must be clearly understood. For example, visualize what it means to "work" and not "steal" for a living! Describe what this person looks like to others, and to themselves? Try to *see* all the values you hold dear clustered together to form character. This is not easy to do, but it is very helpful. Character is not simple, but complex.

You must have a clear picture of what this instilled character looks like and you must be able to role-play it out to the child. Sometimes keeping a daily "emotional" journal will help you see how you are doing in this regard! At the end of the day, write down the events of the day when you "felt" emotional (mad, sad, glad, guilty). Reconstruct the event (time, place, situation, triggers). Re-read yesterday's journal entry. Look for patterns.

A famous Olympic diver was asked how many times he had made a particular dive. He thought a minute and said, "About a thousand....no, about two thousand! Before I actually dived off the board, I visualized it completely in my mind!"

MAPPING OUT THE ROUTE

The first two segments of the "ABC" system explains the process of mapping out what the Bible calls the "way a child should go". You are forming the structure that will take the child to the desired destination: good character! This is when we elucidate the *values* as the tasks to be accomplished in "training up a child" and illustrate what *behaviors* are expected of those who possess the target values.

Illustration: It is much like "building a road" from here to there! The road has boundaries, warning signs, and other accessories to insure a safe passage.

This phase is also where we identify the boundaries between what is "right" and what is "wrong" as we strive toward the set values. Keep in mind, these are subjective values selected by you, the parenting supervisor. You probably gleaned them from your family, significant others, or the community at large. However, you received and adopted them, they are your standards for acceptable conduct. This is the beginning of "Character 101", basic first principles that must be accepted before you proceed.

In the next segment we will discuss how to keep a child "on track" to the destination of "good character". Discipline is the very important element to insure a safe journey for the child.

Discussion Questions:

1) Describe ways families are different.
2) Explain what we mean by "community standards"?
3) What are the religious or community standards upon which the ABC system is built?
4) What do the letters "A-B-C" represent in this supervision system of child development?

5) What is the basic role of a child care supervisor in the ABC system?

6) When a child makes a behavior "choice", describe the two possible natural consequences?

7) Give at least two reasons why a residential child care cottage family is different from a typical traditional family?

8) List three characteristics of a home that is a "safe haven" for children.

9) A child growing up in a "healthy family" ideally, feels _____and _____.

10) In a healthy family rules are _____and _____but _____.

11) Describe the "roles" in a healthy family.

12) Describe how responsibilities are given to children in a healthy family.

13) What does it mean "healthy families allow for individuality" for its members?

14) Explain how communications are "emotionally draining" in a dysfunctional, unhealthy family.

15) Discuss the negatives in an unhealthy, dysfunctional family.

16) What is "missing" in many children coming from unhealthy families is _____.

17) What is the basic responsibility of the child care supervisor under the ABC system of child development?

18) What makes the negative effects of change affect different children differently?

19) What is the strongest single factor for change for a child in care?

20) Discuss the ways you can help your children adjust to the changes they will experience under your care.

21) Explain why boundaries are so important?

22) Describe some "social", or "spiritual", or "gender" boundaries. Why is establishing values so basic to our task in developing character?

Chapter 4

---✦---

CHOICES:
Making Wise Decisions

PARENTING SUPERVISION PRINCIPLES

12 *The first rule in teaching children to choose wisely is to convey basic instruction to them in what is acceptable conduct.*

13 *When parenting supervisors are too strict and harsh, a child learns to fail.*

14 *Children's unacceptable conduct must be managed with corrective discipline.*

15 *Effective discipline supports parental authority, maintains the core values, and keeps the child safe.*

Forming character in children is much like cooking a cake in a convection oven. The cook operates in an environment (kitchen) that is fully equipped with all the structure (cooking range, pots and pans) and ingredients (spices, condiments, etc.) to bake a cake.

The "cook" is in charge, in control, of the process.

The "cook" combines the ingredients according to a tried and proven recipe that, in the past, has produced a sweet cake.

The "cook" has several options in which to cook the cake: bunt pan, cake pan, or black skillet (best for Pineapple-upside-down cake according to my mother!)

The "cook" regulates the <u>heat</u> to produce the desired cake.

The "cook" regulates the <u>time</u> it will take to cook the cake.

A good "cook" knows when to take the finished product out of the oven.

Not a perfect illustration! It does have some flaws, but it also has some valuable merits! Supervising the training of children in many ways is similar to baking a cake. Effective parenting (supervision) is designed to produce children with character who can function successfully in their world as adults. It takes a good recipe of educational ingredients, but it also takes the skill of a "cook" (parental supervisor) to put it all together and control the process. The process is as simple as A, B, C:

A. Define the **acceptable standards,** core values, the target goals, to instill in a child.

B. Use daily **behaviors in the life** of a child to instill those values; and,

C. Supervise acceptable **choices** with corrective discipline based on the core values.

CHOICES: A THREE-LEGGED STOOL

Previously we noted the first two major phases of effective parenting: acceptable values and good behavior choices. The third major phase in developing character in our children is discipline. The complex actions of discipline could be compared to a three-legged stool. The process for teaching our children to make good choices that result in good character includes three very important training modules we might call the "three C's:"

1 **Convey,** teach the basic values a child needs to act with _acceptable_ conduct.

2 **Connect** the child to the parenting supervisor by _showing an example_ of the finished product.

3 **Correct** deviant behaviors _by maintaining_ the structures and boundaries of the family values.

Basic instruction is the first leg of this stool! It is the parenting supervisor's responsibility to teach values and acceptable norms. Basic teaching cannot be left to any other person or an organizational institution (school, church, labor union, boy scouts, football team, etc.).

The Bible gives parents a direct command. Read Deuteronomy 6:6-9:

> **6** _These commandments that I give you today are to be upon your hearts._ **7** _Impress them on your children. Talk about them when you sit at home and when you walk along the road, when you lie down and when you get up._ **8** _Tie them as symbols on your hands and bind them on your foreheads._ **9** _Write them on the doorframes of your houses and on your gates._ (Deuteronomy 6:6-9 NIV)

This is basic **instruction**, which also includes intentionally or purposefully teaching a child about his limitations and obligations, _and_ of the consequences or penalties if these boundaries are violated. This is basic training in what a child "should" and "should not" do based on the target core values of the parents!

In the garden scene of Adam and Eve, the first "children", the instructions were clear:

> *Of every tree of the garden you may freely eat; but of the tree of the knowledge of good and evil you shall not eat, for in the day that you eat of it you shall surely die.* (Genesis 2:16-17)

What about this did they *not* understand? Had God clearly conveyed to them the boundaries and the consequences? They were taught that they could eat (positive reinforcement) from any tree but one! If they violated that boundary, and ate of it, there would be a penalty. They would "surely die"!

What were God's choices when Adam and Eve were disobedient, that is, did not maintain the core values? Only one choice, death! By the way, what "core value" did they violate? The core value violated was a breach of faith, believing whether or not their "supervisor" (God!) was to be believed or not regarding His expectations for them!

Three key words help us understand how instruction leads to acceptable actions. They are *convection, connection* and *correction*. Together they outline the "three-legged stool" of corrective discipline.

CONVEY: TEACHING THE CORE VALUES

The first key word in defining corrective discipline is *convection*. *Convection* is defined as "the process of conveying". Convection is the circular motion that happens when warmer air or liquid -which has faster moving molecules, making it less dense -rises, while the cooler air or liquid drops down. This is the constant, re-occurring part of instruction. Teaching the values is a daily unending process.

In the instruction phase of discipline, supervising parents define the *"content of character"* desired and the *boundaries* (components, limits, rules, structure) in which the values are practiced and the *penalties for violations*. Corrective discipline should be designed to certify two things: the basic value that was violated and to enforce the boundaries between right and wrong. To be effective, the penalties must be congruent with the violation. Parenting supervisors must be fair, just, if they expect good results from corrective discipline. In addition, both the supervisors and the child must understand the following principles that define the discipline:

1   *Values* - character traits we consider important for functioning successfully in our community

2   *Boundaries* - the rules, limits, or "containers of life" for practicing, developing and holding these values

3   *Penalties* - the consistent consequences for violations

Earlier we studied the "core values" or "standards" of conduct that are expected in our family. In some ways this is simply a matter of family choices, but it is usually based on the community norms in general and the immediate supervisors (parents) *values* in particular. In a Christian organization such as Raintree Village, or a traditional Christian family, those norms are based on values from the Bible.

Similar instructions are given to parents in Proverbs 22:6,
"Train up a child in the way he should go,"

And in Ephesians 6:4,

"...bring them up in the nurture and admonition of the Lord."

"*LEARNED*" HELPLESSNESS

Mother was in the middle stages of Alzheimer's disease. I asked her to cook me a pineapple-upside-down cake to take to the family reunion. Nervously, she said she did not want to! I pressed her by telling her I would help her. We went to the kitchen, but she was stumped at every step in the process! She had made hundreds of them, but her dementia convinced her that she could not do it!

"Learned helplessness" can be defined as a learned state produced by exposure to noxious, unpleasant situations in which there is no possibility of escape or avoidance.

In mother's case she was responding from her dementia. However, many children learn to be helpless as a defense against supposed failures. Learned helplessness can be overcome with supervised behaviors based on good choices. Success breeds success! The more a child experiences a sense of achievement and competency, they are more likely to keep on trying.

There are people who rely on *learned helplessness* as a means to cope with negative events happening in their life. Keith Joseph McKean points out that learned helplessness is based on three things:

1   Internal blaming - "It's me!"

2   Global distortion - "It'll affect everything I do!"

3   Stability generalization - "It will last forever!"

Parenting supervisors play major roles in whether or not a child develops learned helplessness. Learned helplessness can develop early in one's life. Therefore, adults need to be aware of how the criticism they use may affect children. If adults are continually using negative criticism, the child will eventually develop low self-esteem. They may just stop trying. This can lead to a child having negative viewpoints throughout his/her life. The type of reinforcement given to the child by the parents can determine whether or not the child will later develop learned helplessness as a coping mechanism for everyday life events. The child may eventually think he/she has no control over these events. The influence of constant negative criticism on children makes them feel that they must have been "bad" children. Therefore, these children believe they are deserving of such negative criticism.

Some research supports the idea that as a child gets older the child feels the negative criticism is based on their lack of abilities, not based on if they were "good" or "bad." Such research indicates that children who have a secure attachment will demonstrate positive self-evaluations whereas children who don't will demonstrate negative self-evaluations.

Norma grew up in a child care facility. She went through school as an academically "challenged" student. As an adult she completed additional education and landed a job at a local university. She remarked about her earlier years: "I thought I was dumb. I was not. I learned that I could do whatever I wanted to!"

THE ELEMENT OF TIME

Instruction requires TIME! Parenting supervisors must spend time with a child to make any kind of difference in that child's development. Most children spend a lot of time watching television, or playing video games rather than engaging in quality time with their supervisors. Six to eight hours each day are spent in school. The "time-lag" under which you work with a child requires that the routine times of a normal day be wisely used. How much time do you spend training your children? Remember, God only works in TIME!

CONNECT: AN EXAMPLE TO MODEL

The second key word in the discipline process is *connection*. *Connection* is defined as that which exists between people when they feel seen, heard, and valued; when they can give and receive without judgment; and when they derive sustenance and strength from the relationship. A child will just naturally pick up the desired character traits when his or her parenting supervisors are their heroes! Respected and loved!

The second leg to this stool is the power of parental modeling...*an example to follow*! Children are notoriously followers! They love "follow-the-leader" games. Parenting supervisors will lose their credibility if they act one way themselves and tell their children to act another. It is very difficult for a parent to teach a child to not smoke, if the parent smokes! If your language is foul, and your words are laced with cursing, you may expect that from your child as well. The Apostle Paul's words to his "son" still ring true:

> *Let no one despise your youth, but <u>be an example</u> to the believers in word, in conduct, in love, in spirit, in faith, in purity.* (1 Timothy 4:12 NKJV)

The deeds we do are stronger sermons for our children than the words we say. However, clear words spoken and congruent modeling by the parents make powerful training for our children!

> *You shall bind them as a sign on your hand, and they shall be as frontlets between your eyes.* (Deuteronomy 6:8 NKJV)

Proper instruction in the core values is important. A child must know what is "acceptable" and what is "unacceptable". It is also crucial that parents "walk the talk" by living good examples before their children.

A famous psychologist, Albert Bandura, developed the theory of Social Learning. He surmised that people learn by watching others. In his famous Bo-Bo doll experiment, he demonstrated how kids learn by watching adults. After witnessing an adult become aggressive with an inflatable doll, the kids began to imitate the behavior and they became more aggressive.

Research has shown that the process of *bonding* between a parent and a child results from consistent loving interactions where a child develops a trust in the parent's willingness to fulfil the child's needs.

CORRECT: DISCIPLINE TO CHANGE

The third key word that is the target of action for supervisors is *correction.* Correction is defined as the actions of changing something to make it right, or correct. That's what supervisors do, they help a child correct behaviors after bad choices have been made.

Thus, the third and final leg in the stool of "training to choose" is *corrective* discipline. Positive discipline begins with the proper instruction in core values and the binding power of a good example; but corrective discipline is required when the boundaries are violated or ignored. Corrective discipline cannot be understated in training children. Although corrective discipline is often considered to be negative, it also provides a sense of security for a child. Everyone, including young children, want to feel that they control their own lives. Effective corrective discipline gives them this assurance.

However, there is more. Children are "C-H-I-L-D-R-E-N" -*children!* Not only are they incapable of living within the limits of the family values, but they are often openly rebellious! Sometimes it is just a matter of immaturity, while on other occasions it is an open challenge to the parental authority and the attached core values.

In the Garden of Eden, the first "children" were told what "not to eat", but *what* did they eat?! *The forbidden fruit!* Was it because they did not understand the instruction, or the consequences? Probably not! The Apostle Paul noted:

> *"For the good that I would I do not; but the evil which I would not, that I do"* (Romans 7:19)

Discipline helps children develop self-control. Discipline is setting limits and correcting misbehavior. Discipline also is encouraging children, guiding them, helping them feel good about themselves, and teaching them how to think for themselves. Here is where the sense of security is most evident.

Why discipline? First, because it supports and maintains the authority (power) of the parenting supervisors! Someone has to be *in charge* for the protection, security and development of maturing children. In time, they will be as matured adults. But, during the formative years it is the parenting supervisors.

Second, corrective discipline maintains the boundaries and rules that protect the core values of the family. The parenting supervisors, natural parents or child care supervisors are (should be!) models of those values. So, both purposes converge on maintaining and supporting the core values of the family. This is the "stuff" for developing basic character!

God not only protected "the tree of the knowledge of good and evil" when he cast the first children out of the garden. He also dignified and certified His right, His authority, as God! It was not just whether or not they would "eat of the tree" again, but also whether or not they would respect his "right" to restrict them from eating of it again!

Corrective discipline targets two desired results:

1) Maintains the *parental authority* – (keep the one who knows the most in charge!)

2) Maintains the *core values* – (supports the tried and true standards, proven by time!)

Corrective discipline certifies the authority of the parenting supervisor, or the law of the land, or God Himself!

Children *do need to know* that the adults are in charge. Good discipline teaches children to respect the adults in charge. However, respect goes both ways, treat children with respect and let them have some control over their lives, and they will respect you and listen to you.

Children learn self-control through the discipline they receive. Effective corrective discipline can help them feel good about themselves, how a person with self-control acts.

And, it continues to maintain the core values of the family. Boundaries that were breached can be repaired. Standards that were lowered can be re-established.

The wise man counsels parenting supervisors:

"Correct thy son, and he shall give thee rest; yea, he shall give delight unto thy soul" (Proverbs 23:13)

This chapter has outlined the larger picture of "discipline" to include instruction, modeling, and corrections. In a later chapter we will study the lurking risk of *discouragement* that can result from abusive discipline. A child must be taught the acceptable boundaries and values of a family. That means the parenting supervisors must discipline, but there are inherent risks.

Effective parenting gets easier as the "cake is cooked!" The rewards for effective parenting usually come after the work is done. Childhood training events, such as discipline, are usually more enjoyable as a memory than as a contemporary action. However, the most beautiful thing in the world for those who form character in children is to see the finished product as an adult.

Discussion Questions:

1) What do we mean by "acceptable standards" or "core values"?

2) How is a convection oven like training children?

3) Explain what "content of character" means?

4) Describe some "penalties" that would be appropriate in correctively disciplining a child?

5) Why would you give "corrective discipline" anyway? What is the reason?

6) Explain the meaning of "example" "bonding" "connection"?

7) Name the three legs of the stool using three c's?

8) Whose responsibility is it to train our children?

9) Describe some of the "acceptable actions" that you would expect of a child?

10) What are boundaries in training a child?

11) Why would "learned helplessness" be a problem in discipline?

12) Why does discipline require "time"?

13) Effective "bonding" includes _____ loving interactions.

14) Explain the relationship of "self-control" and discipline?

15) Give two reasons why we discipline?

Chapter 5

❦

ACCEPTABLE BEHAVIORAL CHOICES*
*The ABC Supervision System for
Character Formation in Children and Youth

PARENTING SUPERVISION PRINCIPLES

16 *Effective parenting requires that the supervisors develop a workable plan of action.*

17 *The plan must encourage the child to make behavior choices based on the values and standards of the family.*

18 *The personal preferences of a child must be the basis for planning effective supervision.*

19 *Effective parenting monitors the behaviors of a child and communicates progress.*

20 *Target dates are important to a child in scheduling changes toward character-building goals.*

This chapter will outline the ABC system as it was developed at Raintree Village. The goal of the system is *to help children form character, a basic core value system that will guide their moral and ethical decisions in life.* The system is designed to assist parenting supervisors *form internal controls* in children by training them to make good choices about their behaviors based on their core values.

The ABC system is about supervision, *parenting* supervision. Effective parenting happens when a supervisor creates for a child a stable, nurturing environment, is a positive role model, and plays a positive and active part in a child's life. Good parenting supervisors provide moral and spiritual guidance with core values, set limits, and provide consequences for a child's behavior. They accept responsibility for the total development of the child and guide the child in making sound, healthy, life decisions through open communication and mutual respect.

The ABC System for training children was developed over a period of several years beginning in the late 1980's on the campus of Raintree Village Children's Home. The training protocol revolved around three critical criteria:

First, acceptable behavior goals (behaviors based on routine core values) were clearly defined and taught. Not only was it important that the acceptable conduct be understood by the child; but the penalties for misbehavior and the rewards for acceptable conduct had to be understood by the child. What was punishing or rewarding for one child may not be for another. Each child must understand these goals based on the child's age, experiences and accepted standards.

Then, a *slow-to-change* process for supervising the child's behaviors was instituted in consultation with the child, the child's peers, and the child's supervisors according to the routine core values of daily living. The System is designed to limit the supervisor's autocratic *one-person-control* over the child's destiny. The System mandated *slow-change* to avoid impulsive knee-jerk reactions by the supervisor or the child.

Finally, the child's positive "good choices" driven by the ABC standards and their "bad choices" which resulted in negative consequences were monitored by the parenting supervisors with privileges or corrective discipline.

In the ABC System the *system* does the disciplining, or corrective punishment. The natural penalties (and rewards) have already been defined to the child before the act of disobedience has been committed! The role-modeling supervisor applies the standards (corrective discipline) according to the disclosures of the individual child for what is "punishing" and what is "rewarding".

Thus, the ABC System is a three-stage plan:

A. *Core Values*: Acceptable goals, core values, for what is acceptable good conduct for a child.

B. *Supervision:* Behaviors supervised and corrected by role models of the core values, the child care supervisors, parents, and others.

C. *Behavior Choices:* Choices with consequences defined by each individual child based on their age, gender, and other considerations.

THE RAINTREE VILLAGE APPLICATION

The following pages provide one example of a formal application of the ABC System as it was developed and is currently used by Raintree Village, a basic residential child care program. This history will give you an idea of how the ABC system developed. The model presented is only an example, you will need to modify the principles to meet the needs of your "family', natural or professional.

The basic philosophy behind the system could be summed up in the following ways:

a) The notion that a child must first know what is expected of him/her, including the acceptable standards of behavior and the attendant rewards and penalties.

b) The child must see and understand a step-by-step plan to "get there" (that is, what the child wants to "be" or, where the child wants to go). The system focuses on two core pursuits of any individual: personal independence and needs fulfillment.

c) The key is that all the behaviors of the child are directly under the effective supervision of an adult (or adults) of sterling character with values that are evident. The parenting supervisors both teach and model the values of the family.

d) This deliberate interactive relationship of the child with the adult (a parenting supervisor) results in forming an internal control of behaviors in the child that will protect him or her and it will serve them well as mature adults. This inner framework we define as *character*.

Essentially, the "acceptable behavior choices" system provides options for young people to choose, with consequences! Freedom of choice is central to the ABC system.

CORE VALUES

The first consideration in forming the ABC system was to define the building blocks for our core values. This process involved making decisions about what is *good* behavior and what is *bad* behavior. These obvious pre-suppositions may seem autocratic, but one assumption of the system is that parents (supervisors) are supposed to *know* (and *practice!*) right from wrong. Values *lived* form the foundation for emerging character.

CONDUCT EXPECTATIONS CLEARLY DEFINED

A child lives in an "adult" world. The adults, via community standards, have decided the rules of conduct including the penalties for breaking the rules, and the rewards for good behavior. These rules, or expectations, are usually learned by the younger generation through the interactions they have with the adults. The values are then passed down, with some modifications, to succeeding generations.

The core values are a *"given"*! The current adult generation, as parenting supervisors, define the core values for the family. However, the core values of one generation must be clearly defined for the next generation, or changed! For purposes of this study they are assumed and accepted as the traditional Judeo-Christian standards of America.

Prior to the ABC System a traditional token system was used at Raintree Village that paid the young people for good behavior, and deducted from their pay for misbehavior. Such a system works as a part of a larger plan, but it implies that money is the only reinforcement of good behavior! Also, some misbehaviors that were most serious for one supervisor was *not* bad at all for another. Thus, it was difficult for a child to see that system as fair. It was based on each supervisors' daily judgment calls.

The punishment, under the token system, was designed to fit the crime. So every person, regardless of age or history, got the same penalty for the same breach of conduct! There was no real *general* standard of "right and wrong", nor any real standard for punishments. Each supervisor, based on his/her personal values and emotional personality, set the standards and inflicted the punishments for misbehaviors.

The prior system had some flexibility, but it usually was entirely up to the mood and personal values of each child care supervisor. Abuse of the system was prevalent, and children were systematically treated unfairly.

EXPECTATIONS OF HOPE, NOT DISCOURAGEMENT!

Restriction was the only punishment regularly used by a supervisor at Raintree Village. A child was typically *restricted* to his/her room for infractions of the rules. The practical result was that, if a child (or supervisor!) had a bad weekend, the only major thing that could be done was to yell: *"YOU ARE ON RESTRICTION FOR A WEEK...THEN TWO MORE WEEKS...THEN FOR THE NEXT MONTH"!*

The child, and supervisor, literally dug a hole so deep that the child had no hope of ever getting out! All in one-week end! In addition, the child was in such a hole that it must have felt like they were on "death row!" So what difference did it make how he or she behaved! Instead of maintaining peace the system resulted in chaos.

Even worse, each child was at the individual mercy of that particular supervisor. Restoring peace to the community seemed to result in only two possible solutions: 1) Discharge the disturbing child to another family setting, or 2) Fire the supervisor! The first solution just passed the problem on to someone else, and the second might have resulted in what could be a very good supervisor. The basic rule for parenting supervision was what was really lost: *Do what is in the best interest of the child!*

So, potentially good parenting supervisors were harassed and many needy children literally fell through the cracks! Everyone was unhappy. The combination of paying for good behavior (tokens) mixed with unfair discipline meted out by frustrated, emotionally-charged supervisors, simply was not working.

FAIR SUPERVISION

The ABC System had to be one in which a child grew and developed in a happy, cheerful way. The parenting environment had to be stable. The parenting supervisors had to rule with benevolent authority. This system had to involve treating each child as an individual, with consideration for their needs, wants, self-wills, emotions, and their futures. The child had to have the power to make choices. *The ABC system treats young people as individuals!* Each child is dignified as an individual person with respect. The mutual respect in the interactions of the supervisors and the children must result in a stable system for solving problems in the community. Treatment for one child may be different than for another, but the system was fair.

SURVEY OF LIKES AND DISLIKES

Second, those of us supervising the conduct of children needed to understand the wants, needs and fears of each child. This would require collecting information directly from each child.

PREFERENCES OF THE CHILD

Throughout the year in 1989 each youth coming into care was given a simple survey asking two major questions: *(See Appendix: Child Survey)*. A child survey for a traditional family may be different from this example. The idea is to find a way for the parenting supervisors to gather the necessary information on a child's likes and dislikes. By focusing on these two categories of preferences parenting supervisors can help the child make good choices. The basic questions are simple:

1)   "What things do you like?" and,
2)   "What things do you *not* like?"

The RTV questionnaire listed all the usual ways a child may be punished and all the usual things a child likes to possess or do. Each questionnaire was graded according to the child's age and gender. The "likes" and "dislikes" were condensed into a graded series of profiles by age and severity. This resulted in forming the ten *supervision conduct levels*.

The Child Survey not only provided valuable information to the supervisor on what was punishing or rewarding for the specific child by gender and age, but it also guided the supervisor on how to be flexible in working with different children in their unique circumstances. This profile allowed us to treat each child as an individual.

These profiles were then analyzed to grade what things were "most rewarding" and what things were "most punishing" for a child considering that child's age and gender. We were looking for the things that might drive or motivate a young person to choose one behavior over another. Parenting supervisors needed to know which button to punch or, to "turn up the heat", that is, to increase the pressures of both positive and/or negative consequences to influence the choices the child would make. Remember, you are the supervisor, the child is the supervisee! You must determine what is *right* or *wrong, good* or *bad,* for each child until that child's inner structure (character) is developed.

The results of the Child Survey were used to develop two tools: the individual child care plans and the formation of the "Supervision Conduct Levels" (*See Chapter 6)* and the "Mode of Maintenance" report *(See Chapter 7).* These two documents became the tools to structure behavior modifications desired in each of the children. They are assessment scales that inform both the supervisor and the child how the training is progressing. The Supervision Conduct Levels gave a visual picture to the child of "where", "when", and "how" that child could enjoy a better life. The Mode of

Maintenance, or M-O-M report became a visual report card to register the child's progress. The next two chapters are devoted to how these tools can be used by parenting supervisors to form the character of a child.

The ABC system uses the self-defined "likes" and "dislikes" of the young person of a particular age and gender to motivate the child to make changes in his or her behaviors. This information is valuable for the supervisor.

Thus, the system of consequences (penalties) and privileges (rewards) of the ABC System resulted. This step in the process helped the supervisor understand what kinds of actions a supervisor might take to be most effective in managing the conduct of a youth at a particular age.

In this system, the child's choices are clearly defined to result in predictable consequences, some negative and some positive.

For example, we learned that to a 15-year-old "talking on the telephone" was much more "rewarding" than it was to a 9-year-old. But, "watching television" was more important to the 9-year-old than the 15-year-old, etc.

A supervisor with this knowledge could use it to discipline a child; however, that supervisor could still arbitrarily administer discipline in an unacceptable, autocratic way.

All this information had to be graded or leveled to provide steps for the child to make progress in acceptable behaviors. Each supervisor had to be limited on what they could and could not do in discipline based on the child's profile. The published supervision levels and the subsequent M-O-M report limited the autocratic actions of an emotional supervisor while giving the child a visual step-ladder to get what he wants--satisfaction and independence!

In review, the system that was to be developed had to be both *age/gender* and *preference sensitive* (what the youth "liked" or did "not like"). In addition, the supervisors' interventions had to be fair and uniform so that the youth could respond with improved conduct.

Penalties and *privileges*, or consequences and rewards, graded and manipulated according to the age and previous behavior of the youth ultimately were divided into the ten (10) gradually ascending supervision *conduct levels.* These ten steps gave the children a visual picture of what they could expect if they made progress to the next levels. The lower levers were weighted heavily with penalties while the upper levels were weighted heavily with rewards.

The idea was to gradually build into the child an internal structure for making choices that would bring more rewards and privileges, and less penalties and restrictions. *These "Supervision Levels of Conduct" became the goals for the child, clearly defined with rewards and penalties in each level.*

SUPERVISION

A third consideration in developing the ABC System was to provide *a gradual, slow-to-change plan of behavior modification,* one that a child could easily understand and become a part of, *while restricting the supervisor's sole control over the child's destiny.*

CONSEQUENCES OF CONDUCT CHOICES

The power of choice, or personal control in the ABC System is programmed to gradually shift from the parenting supervisors in charge to the young person. The shift gradually develops as a child demonstrates his or her ability to make good choices. The "Levels" system is designed to help the supervisors know when to turn loose of some supervision duties. At the same time, the child feels more and more empowered as that child moves up through the levels.

So, decisions that severely restricted a child were taken away from individual supervisors who might have had "bad hair days," or who emotionally became too involved in a particular incident and a particular child. The system was designed to discourage prejudicial treatment of any child.

Actually, the powers of the individual supervisors were reduced as a child grew, developed, and had less need of supervision. In addition, the ABC System expanded the notion of supervision to include other staff, other peers, "the system" and "the village." It was defined to even include the child as his or her internal control structure, and emerging *character*, matured.

REGULAR STAFF REVIEWS

Another expansion of supervision was scheduled staff reviews. Benchmark times, and dates, were needed to both evaluate the child's behaviors and to develop rites of passage for the child to the next level. These were the *staffings* or meetings to discuss and celebrate the child's progress. The idea was to condition a child to look forward to the staff meetings where their conduct level could be changed. And, concurrently, their privileges and independence would be expanded.

Regular periods of time were built in to give each child a *target date* or goal for change at each Level. This would be a meeting on a pre-set date, in which the child, the direct supervisor, and another staff person, and sometimes other members of the family, would evaluate the child's overall conduct in the immediate past.

Then, upon the decision of the group the child may be promoted to the next level (with all the privileges thereto), or demoted to a lower level, or left to repeat the current level. This decision (exercise of power) was made by several people, but brought about by the choices of the child.

A regular staffing (meeting described above) is to build predictable order and routine into the life of the young person. The more a child's life becomes predictable the more likely that child will trust the future.

Remember, the first goal of a parenting supervisor is to help the child become "a believer" ...to trust and become trustworthy!

The regular staffing time is set in advance on a particular date. The child knows this date in advance. He or she knows that they will meet with their supervisors and others to decide whether or not they will move to a higher level. This date is like a "Christmas" or a "birthday"! The staffing dates begin to mold the behavior of the child and serves as bookends to hold things together. Conduct stability results.

The sole result from a staffing meeting in the ABC system is to determine the "conduct level" of the young person.

One of three decisions can be made in the meeting:

1. Leave the young person on their current level with an extension of time until another staffing, or,

2. Promote the young person to the next higher level. This will allow for more, and greater privileges and rewards, and fewer restrictions or penalties.

3. Demote the young person to the next lower level. This will increase the restrictions and penalties and decrease the privileges and rewards.

Emergency meetings could be called by the Social Services professional if necessary. However, the composition of the staffing group still has to include the youth, his/her direct supervisor, and another staff member.

Staffing meetings would most likely be set in advance for a regularly scheduled review. Or, one could be called in the event of an emergency situation. However, the overall purpose of either must be to help the child develop structure, order, stability to his or her life. Disorder creates confusion and misbehavior in a child. Order, or stability, that a child helped to define, results in peaceful conduct growth. The *process* is character developing. Spend time designing and defining the process for healthy outcomes.

MONITORING M-O-M REPORT

The "good choices" and the "bad choices" for each child are monitored by the parenting supervisor and properly recorded on the Mode of Maintenance (MOM) Report. The MOM report provides a measurable statistical picture of the progress made by the child over time. The MOM report becomes a visual reinforcement for continued progress, and a corrective tool for discipline.

SMALL CHANGES IN BEHAVIORS!

Two statistical MOM scores are recorded for each child:

1. A *basic progress scale* (BPS) measures the child against their personal beginning baseline. This score indicates "progress" in character formation. The score is a percentage ratio of the positives on the MOM report. Each child is measured by his or her own individual "base line", not "one-size-fits-all".

2. The *family functioning scale* (FFS) measures the child's conduct against all the other children in the family. The score compares the BPS score of the child with the average score of the entire family. This score will indicate the relative integration of the young person into the cottage family. This is a relational measurement.

The daily behaviors of a typical child are clustered around three social centers of conduct: *personal care, social interactions, and family duties.* These will be discussed later, but in overview they are routine, daily behaviors. Each child should learn to care for themselves, interact socially with others, and to be a responsible member of their respective family.

IMPROVEMENT EQUALS SUCCESS!

The ABC System measures a child's conduct in detailed, small-step, changes. It is designed to *show minimal progress toward the individual child care goals over set periods of time.* The "acts" or "behaviors" that are evaluated are common, "every-day" activities of life common to everyone living in a community, like personal health and hygiene behaviors as well as social interactions with others, including other children and supervisors.

Any positive movement toward the desired goals is defined as "success" regardless of how small.

The penalties and the rewards are not distributed based on the "act" or "behavior" of the young person, but *on the individual child's progress* (defined by Levels). Each *"miss"*-behavior (when they *failed to "trust" the system*) must be evaluated against that particular child's progress, or improvements, clearly defined by their ABC level, age, and their regular evaluations.

For example, if three children that were on Levels 5, 7 and 9 were to commit the same "act" of misbehavior, one might receive more, or less, penalty than the others based on their individual ABC Levels.

This allowed each child to be compared and measured by his/her own attitude, effort, and history. To repeat, the ABC System is not "one size fits all" plan for behavior change! Each child is respected as an individual, but each child must function in groups with other individuals. Thus, the "Supervision Modes" that follow group the individual young people with others of similar conduct.

SUPERVISION MODES

A mode, for purposes of the ABC system is a classification of collected behaviors that seem to group individual young people together because of their similar behaviors and actions.

The Mode classifications have one purpose: *to define the intensity and duration of the supervision the child is to receive from the supervisors.*

Each Mode has several Conduct levels to more clearly define the progress a child is making in the ABC system. The Supervision Modes will be discussed in detail later.

ABC SYSTEM ELEMENTS SUMMARY:

1 CORE VALUES: Define and communicate the core values, expectations of conduct a child is to develop.

2 CHILD PREFERENCES: Information surveys to determine the "likes and dislikes" of each child based on age and gender.

3 SUPERVISION CONDUCT LEVELS: Clearly defined "expectations" for a child's conduct with consequences: rewards and penalties; privileges and restrictions.

4 MOM REPORTS: Accurate documentation, and measurement, of conduct changes by random testing and reporting.

5 STAFFINGS: Fairly administered child's conduct achievement progress meetings set in advance to decide to promote, demote or leave the child on the same Level.

DISCUSSION QUESTIONS:

1) What is meant by a "levels system"?

2) What is the basic philosophy behind the ABC system?

3) _____of _____is central to the ABC system.

4) The ABC system treats young people as _____.

5) What "drives", or "motivates" in the ABC system?

6) How are the Conduct Levels defined?

7) In what way does "restricting" the sole power of the immediate supervisor improve conduct change in a child?

8) Why are there regular, dated staffings in the ABC system?

9) What is the sole result of a staffing?

10) How does the child care supervisor monitor and document the "good choices" and "bad choices" of a child?

Chapter 6

CONDUCT LEVELS:
Setting the Standards

PARENTING SUPERVISION PRINCIPLES

21 *Effective parenting supervisors will work themselves out of a job.*

22 *Remember the golden rule: "treat others (including children) as you would want to be treated".*

23 *Show your child a clear path to success in small steps.*

We all want our children to be safe from harm. As parents we take precautions that will accomplish this for them. However, we all know that we will not always be around for every danger they will face. Therefore, we plan for the time when they are on their own. A time when our parental help is only a memory!

The ultimate goal of parenting supervisors is for children to become independent with *internal behavior control, or* basic character. Our duty is to assist them in becoming productive adult citizens in society with strong resilient characters.   A decision-making framework is developed in the child as he or she successfully imbibes the values of the parenting supervisors. At some point this internal structure must become a real part of the child's own moral character. Daily living will become more and more natural, almost automatic, as the child's behaviors become congruent with the chosen community values. And, the work of supervising them will become less necessary, eventually to end entirely.

This will be the first of two chapters that focus on behavior modification tools parenting supervisors may find useful in moving a child successfully to become a successful adult. A levels system is outlined in this chapter that may be implemented so that a child may *learn obedience*. In the following chapter we will examine a reporting tool, the MOM (Mode of Maintenance) report to chart the progress of a child toward independence.

ASCENDING LEVELS

First, develop a series of steps, or graduation-points from the bottom to the top of a scale. This outline will become the ladder used by your children to succeed. As a child goes up the ladder, they will be developing the internal framework of character. Your children will be learning to organize their behaviors around their values as they make decisions about their conduct. This organizing framework is the makings of their character.

The "Conduct Levels" and "Supervision Modes" of Raintree Village in the *Appendix* outline one framework for charting the progress toward the "internal controls" of character in the child. These levels were developed from the child surveys of RTV children. They work well in a group home setting. A traditional family setting may be somewhat different. The important thing is to visually show a path to success for the child under your supervision.

A family's ascending "Levels Chart" should contain increments of improved behavior. As the behaviors improve by making good decisions, the rewards increase and the penalties, or restrictions, decrease. The message to the child is clear: *Do what you are supposed to do (according to the core values of the family) and you will be happier and have a fuller life experience!* Help your child be successful!

The effectiveness of your "Levels Chart" will depend on how successful you are at visualizing progress toward the desired conduct change! In addition, you must be able to define the progress in minor changes in behaviors, small steps that will lead to the child's goals.

The supervision mode of the child determines both the intensity and the duration of the supervision. Do not treat "all children alike"!

Teens understand the statement: *"You are on restriction!"* They may even understand the "what", "when" and "who" the restriction pertains to! The ABC System suggests that you make it more formal by clustering your "conduct levels" into "supervision" modes. This alerts the child to the fact that your supervision control over them will become restricted by their improved conduct! What parent of teens has not heard the retort: *"Don't treat me like a child!"* implying that your "supervision" mode of them should be different *because* of the child's age! Of course, the typical parental response is often: *"Stop acting like a child and I'll not treat you like one!"*

Even children recognize that there are rites of passage in the way they are treated by their parents as they change! You might use the same "Supervision Modes" applied at Raintree Village (Evaluation, Maintenance, Independence), or label your modes something else. The idea is that the child needs to know that your supervision will be different, restricted as he or she improves in acceptable conduct. (You will notice that

Level 1 of the Evaluation Mode (Probation/Discharge) at Raintree Village may not apply in your planning. This level pertains exclusively to discharging a child in a residential program to some other program). The point is that the progress of a child must be broken into smaller steps and visualized.

Conduct Levels provide structure and order to the child's life. In addition to structuring the improvements in increments, make the levels in timed sequences.

Children today understand that school is divided into "grades" that last for certain lengths of time. They know that when they are "promoted" up it not only means they have done acceptable work, but that the time element was completed. Place a time-limit on each Conduct Level. It may be a school year, but most often it will be a calendar date based on some logical reason (their birthday, or a production at school, or a visit to the grandparents). Children change by "deadline" ...for better or worse! They *do* what they have to *do* by the time it is *due!* That also provides direction, order and stability to their lives.

THE RAINTREE VILLAGE EXAMPLE

The ABC system is designed to help young people develop *internal controls* for acceptable behaviors. *The external controls* (supervision with rewards and consequences) are slowly reduced as a young person slowly develops an internal impulse control system. At the same time, privileges and rewards are gradually increased as the behavior slowly, but surely, changes. Graded improvements are carefully documented by the supervisors in their MOM reports. This evaluation and/or manipulation of privileges and restrictions function for a child in a group of peers of similar behavior histories but is specific to the child and that child's level of conduct.

VISUALIZE IT!

This chapter describes the *levels* of acceptable conduct. The next chapter will focus on the importance of *changing levels* based on the behaviors of the child based on the MOM report. Change, desirable or undesirable, can be charged with anxiety. The following chapter suggests the components, or parts available to the supervisors that bring change about. Change, like every other aspect of effective parenting, should be thought-out and planned by the parenting supervisor.

First, you must set the "baseline" or beginning point for each child in a behaviors framework with other similar children (age, gender, etc.). The standards of behavior for each level are clearly defined for each conduct level. The child must have a clear understanding of how the overall system works and what the levels include.

Second, how a child can change *from one level to another* is defined. The ABC system is built on the notion that more often than not children will make good choices if they understand that it is to their benefit to do so. Thus, each child *must see* his or her "road to improvement" to a higher level *and* be able to *envision* that he or she can achieve it. Your commendations with positive rewards and with positive communications inspire the child to proceed. The child's ability to *believe* in a better future is important. Repeat: BUILD TRUST!

THE CONDUCT LEVELS

(*See* Form 4 in *Appendix*)

The Raintree Village ABC system contains ten (10) classifications of conduct. Each classification, or level, is labeled to define the function of that level from "Probation/Discharge" to "Independence". Each Conduct Level is "time-sensitive", i.e., a child is scheduled to stay in each level a specified time from one week to three years before that child is eligible for a staffing to move to a higher level. Some levels may be repeated.

Each child is initially placed on Conduct Level 4 of the ABC system, the Training level. *The reason for placing anyone new to the program on level 4 is to provide the opportunity for a child to make choices that can either move them up or down.* On rare occasions a child will be placed back into the system after being discharged. In those cases, the child may enter the system on Level 1: Probation/Discharge. That child is actually "on probation". These children can only go "up" to the next level, or "out" to placement elsewhere. Of course this would not be an option in a traditional family setting.

The ten (10) Conduct Levels are clustered around three (3) SUPERVISION MODES. These are discrete groupings that identify the *amount* and *intensity* of supervision needed for each peer-grouping. The amount of supervision may refer to how chronic (time) it should be. The intensity of supervision refers to how acute it should be. The lower levels require that a supervisor be more vigilant (checking on a child more often) and attentive to the child's whereabouts.

CONDUCT LEVELS PLACEMENTS

First, each child is placed on a particular "level" based on that child's past conduct, on the evaluations from the MOM Reports, and upon the recommendation from the "Staffing" of the child. Although the placement is somewhat arbitrary (from Level 1 to Level 10), the placement should allow for either upward or downward movement. Essentially, it means providing the child the *opportunity* to make acceptable choices. *Where* a child starts out can predict the future emotional state of the child.

Repeat, entry level for most young people should be Level-4, which is the highest level in the "Evaluation Supervision Mode". The child care supervisors will then administer oversight and evaluations (MOM Reports) based on the "Level" assigned for each young person.

Since the conduct Supervision Modes inform the supervisor regarding the *amount* and *intensity* of the supervision required all restrictions and privileges are administered according to the specific Supervision Mode of the child. Some restrictions and/or privileges (such as eating out as a group, going on recreation trips, etc.) are available ONLY to the youth who are not in certain Supervision Modes.

At the time a child is placed in an assigned level, two things are identified and explained for the information of both the child care supervisors and the child:

First, the earliest possible date for advancement to the next level is set. Each of the Conduct Levels has a predetermined maximum number of days a child must remain on that level. The durations become longer as the child advances.

It is important that both the child and the child care supervisor understand that the future is structured and predictable. Setting a date for the next opportunity to advance both stabilizes a child's future and provides hope for the child gaining what they desire and more independence.

Second, the exact date for the next level's review is set detailing the additional privileges on the next higher level. This much like dangling a carrot in front of a rabbit! Seeing the rewards at the end motivates the child to achieve.

Thus, a review of the privileges and penalties that go with the next level creates a decision on the part of the child. Personal choice is at the heart of this program. A child can only make a good choice if that child has the information defining the rewards and restrictions associated with certain conduct and conduct levels.

Emergency Staffing Meetings may be scheduled for flagrant violations and/or exemplary conduct. All emergency meetings must be scheduled and called by the Executive Director.

RANDOM EVALUATIONS ON CONDUCT LEVELS

Second, in the ABC System each child is *randomly* evaluated at various times according to his or her Conduct Level. Those who are on lower levels of the Evaluation Mode are evaluated almost daily. The higher levels of Maintenance and Independence Modes may be evaluated randomly every week or even less often.

The evaluation date is scheduled *in advance* for each child, but the child *is not informed* of the date.

The random evaluation schedules are designed to help the young person remain in a stable state, *while gradually changing!*

Random reinforcement has proven to be more effective than predictable regular reinforcement of behaviors in sustaining permanent changes of conduct.

So, not only are there fewer negatives (restrictions) but there are more positives (privileges) for the upper levels. Thus, the pressures of the system encourage movement up, rather than down.

SUPERVISION MODES

The ABC System has three (3) Supervision Modes of Conduct. These are clustered around three general conduct set of levels: *Evaluation, Maintenance, and Independence.* These are general groupings of young people whose conduct histories are similar.

First, the Evaluation Supervision Mode demands the most from the child and requires the most from the child care supervisor. These are the strictest Conduct Levels with the greatest eye-contact-supervision. These are the children under maximum watchful oversight. Parenting a child in the "Evaluation Mode" is hard work!

A written agreement, or contract, is often used with children in the Evaluation Mode. One or two conditions are usually attached that a child *must* meet before moving up to the higher level.

The *Evaluation Supervision Mode* consists of *Four Conduct Levels:*

Level 1- Probation/Discharge:

From this level a child can only go *up* and remain in the current child care living arrangement. Otherwise, the child will have to be turned over to others for daily supervision and more intense watchful oversight.

Level 2- Restriction:

This is actually a *warning* level. When a child falls to Level 2 punishment is more prevalent with severe restrictions. Time-out takes on a new meaning for a child on the Restriction level.

Level 3- Discipline:

Specific personalized discipline is applied that introduces the negative emotional effect of guilt or remorse. Violations of the ethics, standards of conduct, or laws just will not be tolerated. The offending child may really feel the heat!

Level 4- Training.

Level 4 is designed as the entry level for the system. Every new child entering, except for a *returning* child, is entered on Level 4. A returning child may be placed on Level 1 with conditions.

The differences in *acceptable choices* of conduct and *unacceptable choices* are clearly introduced in Level 4. A sampling of both the unpleasantness of the negatives and the happy hope generated by the pressures to move up train the child in *how life works in the real world.* The child is continually reminded that whatever happens in his or her life is a result of choices that child makes. This is the core training pattern for the ABC system.

> *Level 4 is the entry level to allow greater freedom for a child to move up or down. If they were placed on Level 1, the only movement possible would be up!*

Although discipline and training exist on all levels, the Evaluation Mode is especially restrictive, or even punishing in nature. Those who are leveled here experience very close supervision, multiple restrictions, and often evaluations. In addition, their privileges are limited.

No one expects a child to *want to remain* in the Evaluation Mode for very long. The greatest external controls are in place at these levels from "eyesight" supervision to almost daily MOM Reports. The child care supervisors will work the hardest and are required to monitor (with documentation) almost one-on-one the behaviors of the young people in the Evaluation Supervision Mode. Supervising children in the Evaluation Supervision Mode is hard work but if it is done well, the future gets much easier.

The **_Maintenance Supervision Mode_** has three conduct levels. All three are very similar, just more of the same in terms of rewards and restrictions. This Mode is, ...well..MAINTENANCE!

Level 5-Low Maintenance;

Level 6-Regular Maintenance;

Level 7-High Maintenance.

The *Maintenance* supervision *mode* is where most children will be most of the time. We expect them to maintain, remain stable! Each child will be expected to reach and maintain one of the Maintenance Supervision Mode levels within a short time. The child will remain in these three-conduct levels for the longest time. These three levels represent the routine, regular ...*real life* experiences most children face. By the time a child moves into the Maintenance Mode that child has learned the routines, understands the process, and is making progress.

Life in the Maintenance Mode is predictable, stable and sometimes even boring. However, it is in these levels that a child begins to feel safe and secure with a predictable future.

The general population of the family routinely operates in the *"maintenance"* mode. This is *daily* living. You get out of bed, do your normal personal chores, and get ready for the day. A typical day for you has some positives, and a few negatives. Here is where the child learns to "cope" with *real* life. The daily choices focus on small, regular things. There are fewer crisis choices in the Maintenance Mode.

The work of managing the child's choices will be more "routine" and much easier in the Maintenance Supervision Mode than the previous four levels. Supervision is less restrictive and the individuals in this Mode have more freedom of mobility with greater privileges. That's why we expect most of our young people to eventually reach this Mode and stay in it for the longest time. But howbeit more slowly, the child still has room to move up to a higher level. Growth and progress is still the goal.

Finally, the **Independence Supervision Mode** is represented by three conduct levels:

Level 8-Honors:

The real leaders in the cottage should be on this level. These are the peer examples of the finished product...the showroom models of acceptable behavior choices! These are the older, more experienced children who have chained together many good choices over a long period of time.

Level 9-Senior Honors:

When a child has moved up through the educational system and reached their pinnacle senior-year, that child deserves special recognition and independence. Time is running out for the parents, or supervisors, to effect many more changes. Level 9 is reserved only for seniors in high school.

Level 10-Independent Living:

Some might call this level the "intern" level. A child has developed sufficient internal controls that they could almost live alone. These are the older youth who have developed maturity of choices. The supervisors, or parents, become more like *consultants* on this level. Supervision is minimal (rather than very close) due to the ability of the young person to conduct himself/herself in a proper manner with more internal controls.

These are the leaders in the family; but the parenting supervisors must not treat them like *parenting supervisors*! You are still the parenting supervisor, the leading authority in the family. One of the dangers at these levels is "parentification" --children acting as parents!

CONDUCT LEVELS CHANGES

The prevailing task for any child in the ABC System is to move up to a higher level. Three things will change in a child's quality of life when that child is promoted to the next available level:

- MOM Report evaluations will be less frequent with greater hope of remaining stable,
- Privileges/rewards will *increase*,
- Penalties/restrictions will *decrease*

The practical results that come from promotion to higher levels will include more freedom and independence, more money to spend, and many other positive elements that go with the higher level. More of the child's desires will be satisfied.

At the same time "the heat" is turned down as restrictions ease up. The child begins to experience a much more pleasant and peaceful life.

So, both the supervisors and the children under supervision should want every young person to move up to a higher level!

Promoting a child to a higher level *indicates success for the young person* involved. The child has developed stronger internal controls. These young people are making more "good choices" than "bad" ones! Their daily conduct is more congruent with the code of conduct for the family. Measureable improvements are obvious.

Moving up is a celebration of the emergent character being formed in the child.

The supervisors, or parents, also benefit when a child is promoted to a higher level. The higher levels require much less work in oversight of the children. And, life is much more peaceful in the family. In addition, the child care supervisor will have more "examples" to put group pressure on those who still "miss-behave"! One child's progress becomes an encouragement for others to succeed.

PROCEDURES FOR CONDUCT LEVELS CHANGE

The progress, or relapse, of a young person should be closely monitored via the MOM Report to help young people *see* the road to success. Effective parenting always looks out for the best interest of the child. Repeat: *We all want each child to improve and move toward independence!*

Changes from one level to another are *carefully authorized* to promote or demote any young person in the conduct levels system. The procedure has been *purposely* designed so that changes are *slow* and *predictable*! But, *change* is the task for both the child and the parents who supervise.

The authorized procedures for Conduct Level changes at Raintree Village are given as an example of how changes can be done. The point is, the child must be invested *in the process* for it to be successful. So, listed below is a brief summary of the RV protocol for Levels change:

DOCUMENTATION:

Child care records should include the MOM Reports, Case Goals for the child, written supervision logs, and Serious Incidence Reports. If it is not written, it did not happen! The paperwork verifies the work that has been done to bring about change. Documenting case behaviors is also our insurance for any future problems.

A written record becomes valuable evidence in case of a legal issue.

Natural parents may just rely on a *daily log* or a written contract with conditions. The written agreement and the log become significant evidence if severe consequences are required.

CASE REVIEWS:

The Social Services professionals will review each case noting progress toward the child care goals for that child.

Parents in a natural family should keep personal records on each child with age-gender-identification that will include both the goals and the behaviors.

PEER REVIEWS:

The young person, and other young people, may talk with the Social Services professionals to "present their case".

In a family setting the parents may conduct a family council meeting to review a child's conduct. Let each member of the family *testify* to the validity of the needed change.

CASE SCHEDULING:

A specific date is set for the child's case to be heard in a regular staff meeting called for the opportunity for advancement.

A note may be placed on the kitchen bulletin board listing the date a family council will meet to change the restrictions and privileges of a child.

REGULAR STAFFING MEETING:

On the date set in advance, a meeting is conducted with the social services professionals in charge. In addition to the young person involved, the meeting could include one other staff member and the child care supervisors. If the child desires, another resident in care may also be invited to the meeting. In the natural family, the meeting might include others (teachers, coach, etc.) as well as the family members.

DECISION OPTIONS FOR THE STAFFING:

Only three options are possible for the child in a scheduled staffing:

1) Promote to the next higher level,
2) Demote to a lower level,
3) Remain on the current level.

At Raintree Village all level changes must be approved by the Executive Director based on the recommendations of the staff.

In a natural family the parents obviously must make the final decisions to make recommended changes in penalties and rewards.

The authority and the attendant duties of parenting must be maintained to provide order and stability in the family.

PUBLICATION:

Visual and public notice of the change in Conduct Level will be made to all residents and staff at Raintree Village. In cases of a promotion, it might be in order to have a "celebration" ceremony in some way. Downward changes may be noted with a MOM report posted on the bedroom door. The same type publications could also be done in the natural family.

EMERGENCY STAFFINGS

A Conduct Level change can be made under certain conditions through a called *"Emergency Staffing"* meeting. This meeting must be called by the Executive Director upon recommendation from the Social Services professionals. Assigning this important decision to the chief executive officer of the organization alerts the child to the fact that this is serious business.

Emergency Staffings are limited to certain violations (demotions) and/or exemplary behaviors (promotions) of young people. These conditions might include, but not limited to, crimes committed, sexual violations, running away, flagrant violations of curfew, etc. *Emergency Staffings* (prior to the date for a regular staffing) for promotions might include unusual progress toward child care goals, exemplary conduct in a crisis, and other out-of-the-ordinary behaviors that are exemplary.

Thus, all *Emergency Staffing* results must be approved and authorized by the Executive Director. The important thing is to make it a little more difficult to call such a meeting. It really *must* be an emergency!

FAIR AND IMPARTIAL JUDGMENTS

The ABC system is designed to protect the individual young person from arbitrary censure or demotion. A child should not lose everything (privileges, level status, etc.) just because of a "one bad day" ... for either the supervisor, or the child! The system is designed to work slowly, with small steps forward, so that a child will not become discouraged, and lose hope!

However, having said that, some acutely dangerous behaviors, may need to be handled in the sole discretion of the administration with or without Staffing Meetings as outlined above. The same is true with natural parents. Some decisions are solely the responsibility of the parenting supervisors.

Discussion Questions:

1) Why would any child want to go up in the Levels system?

2) What increases when a child is demoted to a lower level?

3) Explain how a child care supervisor benefits when a child is promoted to a higher level?

4) When a child moves up, _____ controls are decreased and _____ controls are increased?

5) We all (staff and children) want them to move toward _____.

6) True or False? The procedure for changing levels is slow and predictable.

7) True or False? A child care supervisor, in consultation with one other social service professional, may demote a child for bad behavior.

8) True or False? The date for regular staffings should be set two weeks prior to the Staffing meeting.

9) The final decision for (conduct level) change will be made by the _____.

10) True or False? Other children should never be in the meeting when a level change is being considered.

11) Discuss when, under what conditions, an "Emergency Staffing" can be held?

Chapter 7

—⊱✦⊰—

M-O-M REPORT:
Maintaining Right Conduct

PARENTING SUPERVISION PRINCIPLES

24 *Acceptable behaviors performed by a child on a daily basis will result in the conduct becoming a good habit.*

25 *Children develop inner self-confidence from a sense of belonging and achievement that is noted and celebrated by their parental supervisors.*

The ABC system is based on the belief that people will not willfully harm themselves. Nor will a mentally healthy person purposely do something that will make them unhappy. We all need positive reinforcements for our good choices. So, it is important that parental supervisors visually communicate a child's progress.

This chapter proposes communication tools parenting supervisors can use to encourage progress in a child's character formation. Specific things you can do are suggested, but the most effective tools are the ones you will develop. Think of ways to communicate to your child that they are making progress. Think in small units, not grand patterns. Communicate and celebrate the smallest step toward the desired goals.

First, develop a score card documentation that will visualize the family core values, supervise the child's behaviors, and publicize the child's progress.

In the ABC system we call this the MOM report. This is an acronym for the **Mo**de **Of** **M**aintenance or, the MOM report.

Two elements upon which character is formed are visualized by the MOM Report: *core values* and daily *behaviors* related to those core values. The core values are the TAGS, the target expectations and goals for acceptable conduct. The second element includes modeling those core values is a record of daily behaviors. Another way to say it is that we hold certain values and we practice them.

A compact definition for "character" may be "a core values framework modeled by repetitive behaviors."

Good character is good because good core values are practiced. Bad character is poor core values practiced.

The MOM report, to some extent, measures the congruent progress of these two values in forming character in a child. I am not proposing that the actual character of a child is defined by the MOM report. Rather, the ability of the child to act responsibly in daily living according to good core values is measured.

I am proposing that the formation of the *character framework* is the internal process of the interaction between personal behaviors and internally-held values. Supervision by adults manage and monitor a child's behaviors in comparison with the TAG values established by the family or community. Parenting supervisors are essentially training a child to be a *good* citizen.

"Good" citizenship, at least according to the Judeo-Christian core values upon which the Raintree Village model was based, include many daily behaviors. Some of the more common ones are listed on the RTV MOM report attached in the *Appendix*. These routine core values center around three clusters of daily behaviors:

1) The child's personal care behaviors
2) The child's social interactions others
3) The child's behaviors and duties to the family and community

Second, visualize and communicate the child's progress in moving toward independence and self-control by making good choices.

A parent's greatest satisfaction is in training a child to be independent, self-controlled with values that equate to "good" character as defined by the core values of the parents, or supervisors! This is made possible for the child as he or she develops successful life patterns. You either help the child make life a series of habits, repetitive behaviors, that are good and healthy; or, a series of bad habits that create chaos and disorder. The results of our work as parenting supervisors is either a joy or a sorrow, depending on our success or failure in training our children to make good or bad choices.

> *In the ideal world, the child will develop according to the standards and values of the parents, but will eventually become his or her "own person."*

This confident place of independence, autonomy, should be the ultimate goal in the character development process.

Good, successful, achieving life patterns produce confidence and healthy self-esteem. Parenting supervisors *train* a child to make good choices a daily habit. Bad choices are punished, or corrected, so that the child continues on a pattern of success. The independence and basic character of the child develop from three components of a healthy self-esteem:

1) Personal competence, or achievement,
2) A sense of belonging, being a contributing agent to the family or society,
3) A belief of self-worth, or personal value.

The child may select other core values when that child has gained ultimate independence from the parenting supervisors. Or, the parent-instilled core values may be modified over time as the child continues to grow and change.

However, the baseline in effective parenting is the core-values of the parenting supervisors' as natural parents, adoptive parents, or professional parenting supervisors. Later generations have the inherent freedom to change values, but only after understanding and practicing the family-community values of the current generation.

Third, parenting supervisors must monitor the child's conduct based on the values and expectations of the family.

Supervision! Supervision! Supervision! One of the saddest scenes in our world is to see children totally without adult supervision. In the extreme we might call them "street children", or worse still "orphans". Left to themselves such children will emulate the lowest standards of survival. The core- values they model often are deviant and socially odious. Thus, the ABC System envisions a child *"under supervision"*.

Parents are expected to be the parents, and children are expected to be children!

The daily conduct of a child is always the direct responsibility of adult supervisors. Sometimes it is total eye-sight maximum oversight supervision such as a young child on a playground. Later, it is supervision through trust and information as an older teen "calling home" to report in.

Parenting supervisors must monitor every aspect of a child's behaviors, particularly when they are young. This takes time and patience. It is not easy. But children must be supervised.

However, if the saddest thing is to see street children with no supervision, a close second is to see older teens who are smothered in supervision --lacking trust! As children grow, they are in need of less supervision and more freedom. The over-arching force must still be *core values* but the application of these values is age specific.

Parents must learn to *take hold* of the behaviors during the early years, and to *turn loose* as the child grows older.

Fourth, find ways to visualize, publicize and celebrate small changes in a child's behaviors toward the desired goals.

Effective supervisors make the smallest progress forward a reason to encourage the child while major changes are highly celebrated. By doing so, the parenting supervisor is confirming the values of the family to the child and commending the child for behaving in accordance with them.

Now, study the Raintree Village MOM Report that follows (Appendix) to help you formulate your own "score card" instrument (MOM Report) that will translate your core values into daily individual behaviors in the children you supervise.

THE MODE OF MAINTENANCE REPORT

The ABC System is a *system,* an organized approach to help children for a healthy, good character framework. Each part of the system affects (emotionally and behaviorally) all the other parts in the system. Each child, the supervisors, the structure of the living unit, the application of rewards and penalties, the supervising administration, and the basic core values all perform in unison as integral parts of the total system. The system operates efficiently and smoothly when this happens. There is balance and peace with progress. Children with good character can survive in a hostile world. That's our goal: strong children, strong adults!

We do not want to lose a single young person due to discouragement, deviant behaviors, or even death. More precisely, my goal is to develop the internal decision-making-power each child needs to have a quality life.

This power I define as basic character formed around core values by making good choices about personal behaviors.

A child's daily social and interactive process is the platform for this to take place. Based on these assumptions four principles frame the tasks of the parenting supervisors:

1) To instruct and model the basic core values of the community in general and the supervisor in particular,

2) To manage and monitor the process of successful life choices defined by the values,

3) To support and/or correct social interactions

4) To celebrate acceptable conduct in a safe, healthy living environment

These four concepts form the basis of evaluation, documented on the MOM Report, for change in a child. All the forces of the system (rules, supervision, privileges and penalties) focus on each child to accomplish the changes desired. Each part, working with all the others, can result in conduct change for a young person. All four of the principles must work in unison to produce healthy character in a child. *Your task is to supervise this process.*

A DAILY PROCESS

The *acts* or *behaviors* evaluated on the MOM Report are clustered around three topical areas of daily life. These are common, everyday behaviors.

> *A fundamental belief of the ABC system is that if a child learns to make good choices about little things (eating, sleeping, school, etc.) then that child will develop the framework-ability to make good choices about big things!*

Children in healthy families achieve their sense of value and worth based on their performance of these simple tasks:

Personal Care:

These behaviors pertain to such things as body care, eating and sleeping care, personal hygiene, physical exercise and personal study habits.

Social Responsibilities:

Communications, social interactions, sexual conduct, conduct at school and church, use of the telephone and internet, general safety, and common manners comprise this cluster of behaviors.

Family Duties:

A child must learn to do his or her part as a member of the family. These behaviors involve daily chores, general room care, bed- meal-time behaviors, respecting authority and other's space, and interpersonal talk.

Don't look for the big things, but focus on the daily little things! This is where training occurs in the child. Routinely! Daily! Small changes in conduct!

A HEALTHY SELF-CONCEPT

First, we want our children to feel good about themselves. A child's self-concept is his or her belief about how worthwhile he or she is. It is how that child sees himself, or herself. Self-esteem is made up of a sense of belonging and being accepted, a sense of being good, and a sense of being capable of doing well.

These qualities of the self-concept of a young person develop in his or her personal relationships and interactions with others. The more important, or significant the other person is to the young person, the more likely they are to have an impact on the child's self-concept, either negatively or positively! Such people are referred to as *significant* others. They may be friends, or enemies, teachers, coaches, siblings or any other person perceived by the child as significant. This would certainly include those who parent, or supervise the child.

We come to understand *who we are* (self-concept) and *what we are worth* (self-esteem) as we look into the faces and listen to the words of the *significant others* with whom we interact ...those who are important to us! Our parents! Our heroes! Our friends and our enemies...everyone! This interaction process is what you must supervise.

The reactions of others to our appearance, cleanliness, grooming, and other personal care tasks impact our own self-esteem. On the other hand, when we think we are "O.K.", others tend to reinforce that belief. The interaction between supervisor (you) and supervisee (your child) is the structure of the process that produces character.

SUCCESSFUL LIFE PATTERNS

The second goal in helping a child develop character is to equip the child with achievement, success in life situations. We want to help the child string these successes together so that *success patterns* begin to become normal, even *habitual*. However, a child's "string of successes" will always be broken by failures. That's when a parenting supervisor's training methods become critical to the child's development. How a supervisor reacts to such failures, and with whatever emotions are attached, tends to galvanize either more success or more failures. Remember, *stability of life* is essential for healthy character formation!

> *Ironically, a child needs to feel safe while making healthy choices, but crisis situations in which they do not feel safe is where the ability to make good choices develop!*

The key component in this process is effective parental supervision. In times of trouble, a child (or, even an adult!) will turn to those they trust. Supervisors who have taught children how to believe, to trust, will maintain a lifetime bond.

The MOM Report identifies the areas of life where successes are possible: in the family, at school, in the dining hall, within the structure of the daily routines, on the school bus, or in personal relations with others. It is also the scorecard, the tally-sheet, for each child's progress. *Each time a child gets a plus (+) for a common, everyday activity, that young person is successful...even if it is just in a common thing like going to bed on time!*

However, making "bad choices" can become a habit also. The MOM report helps the young person break that habit, and begin the habit of good choices. Good choices based on core values is an act of success, achievement, for the child. This builds inner strength and power.

The goal of the MOM report is to help the child string successes together over time and for the child to <u>see</u> the results!

APPROPRIATE SOCIAL INTERACTIONS

The MOM report records simple behaviors like common courtesies to much more serious issues like sexual misconduct. Respecting the property of others, and respecting authority are matters of learning appropriate social interactions. This does not mean the simple issues and the more serious issues should be treated as equal. They are not, at least in terms of the consequences. But the MOM report does provide a way of measuring conduct change in a child with a diverse set of behaviors. Again, this system focuses more on the *process* more than on the *content* of the behaviors. Inappropriate sexual conduct is certainly not the same as not brushing your teeth even though they both merit only a check-mark (x) on the MOM report.

These are behaviors that help a child live in a group, a community, with other people. The young person has to learn that his or her needs-fulfillments are directly tied to how he or she helps others fulfill their needs! This builds social unity based on shared values. These skills would not be essential for someone who lives as a hermit, all alone; but, they are critical to us who live in a community with others. In fact, if a child does not develop these social skills, that child locks himself into a life of friendlessness and loneliness. Such isolation often results in other more serious mental disorders.

SAFE, HEALTHY LIVING ENVIRONMENTS

A basic duty of parenting is to provide for the safety and health of each child. The MOM report identifies what our social needs are and how to be safe and healthy in the larger community. This could include such things an unsanitary living situations as well as dangerous unsafe conduct. A child's safety depends on both the environment and the behaviors of those in the environment.

Remember, our training as parenting supervisors is so that the child may "live long on the earth".

Specific line items on the MOM report document respect for authority, physical and property violence, as well as cleanliness of room and even (negative) communications. The everyday good, bad and the ugly behaviors of our children should be captured on the MOM report.

The Raintree Village MOM report is based on the Judeo-Christian values, morals, and behaviors that are generally acceptable according to the community standards of typical America communities today.

Thus, the mission of the ABC System is to help young people instill in their conducts the ability to function as valuable productive citizens in an America based on the values of the typical American community.

A STRATEGIC FAMILY SYSTEMS APPROACH

In addition, the ABC System comes from a *strategic family systems* approach based on the integration of various parts into a systemic whole. Any systems approach is concerned with the big picture, the sum of the parts working together. Guiding systemic principles for the ABC System are:

Strategic, which refers to the *use of power*, or control in a system based on family. The "power" for the supervisors is the structure of the system. The "power" for the youth is the right to choose behaviors which can result in either positive or negative consequences.

Systems refers to the fact that many parts must work together, in teamwork. All youth care supervisors, both direct child care supervisors and professional supervisors, must work in cooperation with the youth for success.

Family connotes the pattern model of "mom-dad-and-the-kids", the basic traditional family. However, the "family" in a residential child care cottage is not a traditional family. But, the role of authority and the social interactions of the members are patterned after the traditional family.

In many ways the ABC System functions as a closed structural family system. Our families operate as a world-within-a-world. They are bounded by the laws of the state regarding training children on one side, on the other side by the codes of conduct established by the social norms in the community in which we live. Each specific family operates with some rules and policies that are different from some other families. However, the larger community standards, rigid as they are, provide the base. Our personal families should not be isolated from the world around us.

Personal *power to choose* is the behavioral component that makes it work. This closed structure operates by "choices", "consequences", "restrictions" and "privileges". A child's character will be formed *in the process* of making such choices.

If personal choice is denied the child will become either a walking autocrat, a zombie, or a rebel.

Our task is to develop the framework for independent choice and acceptable choice conduct.

SUMMARY OF THE MOM REPORT:

The MOM report is a generic evaluation tool used for two purposes:

A. To define some of the core values for expected behaviors under the categories of "Personal Care", "Social Responsibilities" and "Family Duties";

B. And to report the child's progress for both the child's benefit and the parenting supervisors' guidance.

In conclusion, notice some key points about the MOM REPORT. These are based on operant behavioral conditioning designed to keep the supervisors in charge as the child is evaluated.

1) Frequency of a MOM Report

Progress reports on a child's behavior should be *randomly,* not predictably provided. Patterns of behavior are more resilient and less likely to extinguish if the behaviors are randomly reinforced according to operant conditioning behavioral psychology.

Thus, the MOM report, as a reinforcement tool to help children change, is administered randomly based on the level of conduct of the child. The child's conduct will be evaluated, but not on a *regular predictable* basis.

For example, Conduct Level 3 is a "Discipline" level in the "Evaluation Supervision Mode". Children in this Mode and Level are evaluated with a MOM report five (5) days out of seven (7). On the other hand, the higher Conduct Level 8 is an "Honors" level in the "Independence Supervision Mode". Children in this Mode and Level are evaluated only one (1) day every fourteen (14) days. The higher the level, the less a child will receive an evaluation.

2). *Random Dated Evaluations*

Each child is also scheduled for these random evaluations (completion of a MOM Report) on a particular date based on their Conduct Level and Mode *in advance*!

For Example: "Billy Smith, who is on Conduct Level 8, during September will be evaluated on Thursday, September 8 and Monday, September 26." However, "Suzie Brown, who is on Conduct Level 6 (a lower conduct level) will be evaluated on Monday, the 5th and Wednesday the 7th, and again on Tuesday 13th and Thursday, the 15th."

Exact dates are chosen ahead of time and scheduled prior to any other information except Conduct Level! However, the exact dates for evaluation are not revealed to the child being evaluated. Thus, the child cannot "pick-and-choose" when to be good, to get a satisfactory MOM report.

3) *MOM Report Posted*

Following the evaluations, the MOM Reports are posted on the door, or bulletin board, for all to see. This public posting can be either a "reward" or a "penalty". This is another example of the child making a "choice" that is restrictive or rewarding. It also shows the importance of a child having the power to choose.

4) *Scoring the MOM Reports*

The MOM report for each child can be maintained via the internet on the website of Raintree Village, Inc. The MOM reports are computerized for statistical purposes. A ratio, or percentage number, is generated based on the pluses (+) and the minuses (-) recorded on the MOM form. The result is a measurable "scale score". This scale score is labeled "basic progress scale (BPS)". It is based on a baseline score for each child. A second scale score measures the position of each child against all the other children in the cottage. This standard deviation score is called the "family functioning scale (FFS)".

For example: If a MOM report for Susie has 27 pluses (+) and 10 minuses (-), she will have a BPS .73. (The total pluses *divided by* the total of both (+) and (-) scores). The BPS score is a ratio of pluses to the total evaluation points.

The FFS score measures the progress of the child in comparison with all the other children in the family. If the *mean* (M) BPS score of all the family members is .61, then Susie has a score of FFS +9; meaning that she is nine points above the average in her family. If she happened to have a BPS of .61 and the *mean* score of the family member's BPS was .73, then she would have an FFS score of -9 meaning she is nine points below average in her family.

Both the BPS numerical notation and the FFS scores simply provide a means of computerizing the progress of a child in very small increments. They do not represent "failing" or "passing" scores. The goal in every case is to show progress.

5) Learning to Make Good Choices

Young people in the ABC System *become empowered* by their acceptable choices. Choices that are optional, but will be either restricting or rewarding! Good choices, or bad choices! The results of those choices are documented with the MOM report. Thus, when character is formed in a child, it is represented by the core values of that child being exercised in a chain of behaviors, which have become a habit. The redundancy of the behaviors both support the core values and give the child the power to choose wisely.

Discussion Questions:

1) What are the four concepts (goals) that form the basis for the MOM evaluations?

2) Name the three categories of the MOM Report?

3) Describe how a child develops his self-concept?

4) Define "self-esteem".

5) What are the three components in forming self-concept in a child?

6) What does the MOM report identify and measure in regard to the child's behaviors?

7) Discuss the goal of the MOM report?

8) A basic duty of child care is to provide for the _____and _____of each child.

9) What is the source of the "values, morals, and behaviors" upon which the MOM report is based?

10) The ____of the ABC system is to help young people instill the ability to make ___ ____ for their lives.

11) The ABC system works as an _____ _____ _____ approach based on _____.

12) What does "strategic" refer to?

13) Describe the behavioral component makes the ABC system work?

14) What are the two purposes for making the MOM report evaluation?

15) How frequent should a MOM report be made on a child? What does the frequency depend upon?

16) Why do we use "random" evaluations in the MOM reports?

17) What determines when a child will receive a MOM report evaluation?

18) Why are the MOM reports posted for all to see?

19) Discuss how the MOM evaluations "empower" the young person to take control of his or her life?

Chapter 8

DISCIPLINE
and Discouragement!

PARENTING SUPERVISION PRINCIPLES

26 *The abuse of parental authority and ineffective discipline can discourage a child.*

27 *Discouraging a child destroys their inner strength of self-esteem and confidence.*

28 *A discouraged child is at risk for alienation and numerous deviant behaviors.*

29 *Alienation is caused by destructive relationships, hostility, learned irresponsibility, loss of purpose or direction, and a failed parenting supervision system.*

Previously we noted the primary results of effective discipline is 1) to establish the authority of the parenting supervisors, 2) to teach and/or maintain the core values of the family and community. *And more importantly, to keep the child safe!*

This chapter will focus on a special danger when parental authority is exercised during the corrective discipline of a child: *discouraging, or breaking the spirit of the child!* Later, we will review child abuse as a second risk that parenting supervisors must face.

DISCOURAGING THE CHILD

First, the destructive power of discouragement will be noted. Then, we will look at some of the primary sources for discouragement for a young person.

Discouragement is both the emotional climate and the motivational impetus for disobedience, delinquency, and social dissonance in young people. It is the continuous put-down a young person feels as a result of his or her communications and interactions with his or her most significant others, especially negative emotional abuse from their parenting supervisors.

Clinically discouraged young people have "lost heart", they have "broken spirits". Much of their acting-out and experimentation with various deviant lifestyles reflect this discouragement. All parenting supervisors *must believe* that there is a *good child* in every *bad* child. Never is it acceptable to purposely make a child feel worthless, or useless, or hopeless! Parenting supervisors should imbue *courage* not discouragement.

DISCOURAGEMENT IS DESTRUCTIVE

The following sketch may be attributed to Charles C. Finn. When I first heard it read at a child care conference more than thirty years ago it was attributed to "unknown author". It appears to describe a particular young person, but it could be any young sixteen-year-old girl, but especially one living in foster care. The poem vividly describes the pain inflicted by discouragement. Listen to the heart of this damaged child within as you read her story!

—❧—

"THE CHILD WITHIN! PLEASE LISTEN TO ME!"

Don't be fooled by me. Don't be fooled by the face I wear. I wear a mask. I wear a thousand masks, masks that I am afraid to take off, and none of them are me.

Pretending is an art that is second nature with me, but don't be fooled, for God's sake, don't be fooled. I give you the impression that I am secure, that all is sunny and unruffled within me as well as without that confidence is my name and coolness is my game, that the water is calm and I am in command, and that I need no one.

But don't believe me, please... My surface may seem smooth, but my surface is my mask, my ever varying and ever concealing mask.

Beneath lies no smugness, no complacence. Beneath dwells the real me in confusion, in fear, in aloneness. But I hide this. I don't want anybody to know it. I panic at the thought of my weakness and fear of being exposed. That's why I frantically create a mask to hide behind a nonchalant, sophisticated façade, to help me pretend, to shield me from the glance that knows. But such a glance is precisely my salvation, my only salvation. And I know it. That is, if it is followed by acceptance, if it is followed by LOVE.

It's the only thing that can liberate me from myself, from my own self-built prison wall; from the barriers I so painstakingly erect. It's the only thing that will assure me of what I can't assure myself, that I am really something. But I don't tell you this. I don't dare. I am afraid to. I'm afraid your glance will not be followed by acceptance and love. I'm afraid you'll think less of me, that you'll laugh, and your laugh would kill me; I'm afraid deep down I'm nothing, that I'm just no good and that you will see this and reject me. So I play my game, my desperate, pretending game, with a façade of assurance without, and a trembling child within.

And so, begins the parade of masks, the glittering, but empty parade of masks. My life becomes a front. I idly chatter to you in the suave tones of surface talk. I tell you everything that is nothing and nothing that is everything, of what's crying inside of me. So when I'm going through my routine, do not be fooled by what I am saying. Please listen carefully and try to hear what I am saying, WHAT I WOULD LIKE TO BE ABLE TO SAY, WHAT FOR SURVIVAL I NEED TO SAY, and BUT WHAT I CAN'T SAY!

Don't be fooled by me. Don't be fooled by the face I wear. I wear a mask, I wear a thousand masks, masks that I am afraid to take off, and none of them are me.

I dislike hiding, honestly, I dislike the superficial game I am playing, the superficial phony. I'd like to be really genuine and spontaneous and me, but you've got to help me. You've got to hold out your hand even when that's the last thing I seem to want or need. Only you can wipe away from eyes the blank stare of the breathing dead. Only you can call me into ALIVENESS! Each time your kind and gentle and encouraging, each time you try to understand because you really care, my heart begins to grow wings, very small wings, very feeble wings, but wings.

With your sensitivity and compassion and your power of understanding, you can breathe life into me. I want you to know that. I want you to know how important you are to me. Now you can be the creator of the person that is me if you choose. PLEASE CHOOSE. You alone can break down the wall behind which I tremble; you alone can remove the mask; you alone can release me from my lonely prison. So don't pass me by. Please do not pass me by. It will not be easy for you. My long conviction of worthlessness builds strong walls. The nearer you approach me, the blinder I might strike back. It's irrational, but despite what books say about a person, I am irrational. I fight against the very thing I cry out for.

But I am told that love is stronger than strong walls, and in this lies hope. MY ONLY HOPE! Please try to beat down my wall with firm hands, but gentle hands, and a gentle heart –for my child is VERY SENSITIVE. Who am I, you may wonder? I am someone you know very well. (Author Unknown)

When a Child loses heart, he or she becomes *discouraged!* Discouragement is a self-made prison where anger, hostility, worthlessness and lack of hope dwell. The first task for the parenting supervisor is to identify and encourage "the child within"! Unfortunately, numerous labels are used to tag the discouraged child as *"aggressive or anxious, attention-disordered or affectionless, unmotivated or un-teachable, as drug abusers or dropouts."*

Urie Bronfenbrenner described it like this: *To be alienated is to lack a sense of belonging, to feel cut off from family, friends, school or work.* More than anything else, a discouraged child feels alone and isolated. They typically add to their misery by blaming themselves. And, in a real sense such discouraged children do not even believe they belong to this planet!

How do we do our work of parenting with children, or youth, who are so "at risk" by discouragement? Actually, all parenting supervisors are asked to work with such young people --at the risk of becoming "at risk" ourselves! We also may become discouraged by the very idea of failing. But, as in too many cases, the children are the losers in both cases.

CHILDREN AND DISCOURAGEMENT

Children suffering from discouragement may be described in the following ways:

They are Angry:

Life for these young people has not been "a bowl of cherries!" Anger eats like a cancer, and ultimately destroys a person. Eric Hoffer described it well,

> *The remarkable thing is that we really love our neighbor as ourselves: we do unto others as we do unto ourselves. We hate others when we hate ourselves. We are tolerant toward others when we tolerate ourselves. We forgive others when we forgive ourselves. We are prone to sacrifice others when we are ready to sacrifice ourselves.*

An angry young person has trouble hiding it! Fredrick Buechner tells us why:

> *Of the Seven Deadly Sins, anger is possibly the most fun. To lick your wounds, to smack your lips over grievances long past, to roll over your tongue the prospect of bitter confrontations still to come, to savor to the last toothsome morsel both the pain you are given...*

IT IS ENJOYABLE! We "feel good" when we "feel bad" when we are angry!

They are fearful:

Too often their demons are real...at least to them! Their fears and suspicions, and even their nervous responses that make them dodge every time they feel threatened, are because of their past experiences! Dorothy Thompson said it well: "Fear grows in darkness; if you think there's a bogeyman around, turn on the light." It's not unusual for these children to want to sleep with the lights on at night.   Many of their fears result in mental disorders as adults.

They are disconnected:

These children are living isolated lives.   Each feels alienated from everyone of "significance", particularly their family and friends.   They feel all alone.   Their loneliness becomes the prison of their despair.

They are troubled:

A troubled child is confused, even bewildered, by life. Nothing seems to make sense.   Everything takes on the aura of danger or pain or threat.   A troubled child is like a caged animal pushed into a corner...they often fight just to survive!   Their lives are filled with turmoil, not peace.   Emotionally, they can even become paranoid.

They are Oppositional Defiant (ODD):

Oppositional Defiant Disorder (ODD) is a mental illness in which children ignore or defy adults' requests and rules. They may be passive, finding ways to annoy others, or active, verbally saying "No!" They tend to blame others for their mistakes and difficulties. When asked why they are so defiant, they may say that they are only acting against unreasonable rules. They are different from children with conduct disorders (CD) in that they do not violate the rights of others. These behaviors are present at home, but not usually in other situations, such as school, or with other adults. Although they may exhibit rebellion in most other social situations.

These children display a low self-esteem, mood changes, low frustration tolerance, and temper outbursts. Many of the children in foster care may suffer from Attention Deficit Hyperactivity Disorder (ADHD).   Just about all of them will, at some time, manifest conduct disorders as well.

Most, if not all, childhood mental and behavioral disorders spring from discouragement, or a sense of lost-ness. That's why it is so important to avoid discouraging a young person.

The Bible speaks about how parental abuse can lead to a child losing heart, or becoming discouraged! A father is charged by God to be the "head of the family" ...sounds like *authority!* Good fathers (and other parenting supervisors!) must discipline bad conduct. However, because of their power and position they run the risk of being too harsh in their discipline! Bad fathers may just vent their own frustrations on the child! Abuse can result in the discipline-process. Notice what the Bible says about this:

Fathers, do not provoke your children to anger, but bring them up in the discipline and instruction of the Lord. (Ephesians 6:4 New King James Version)

Fathers, do not provoke your children, lest they become discouraged. (Colossians 3:21 New King James Version)

Fathers, do not exasperate your children, so that they will not lose heart. (Colossians 3:21 American Standard Version)

Fathers, don't frustrate your children. If you are too hard to please, they might want to quit trying. (Colossians 3:21 Easy-to-Read Version)

Fathers, don't aggravate your children. If you do, they will become discouraged and quit trying. (Colossians 3:21 New Living Translation)

Mark the words used to describe the child: "anger", "exasperation", "frustration", "lose heart", "discouraged", "quits trying"! These terms often describe the children who come from homes with abusive discipline.

Sometimes well-meaning parenting supervisors are too aggressive in applying discipline. Abuse in disciplining a child is especially a risk for those who have the *parenting authority* of *supervision*. Conversely, the broken spirit may come from a learned sense of helplessness as defined in the previous chapter from abuse or neglect. Again, in either case, the child who becomes discouraged is the loser.

THE SOURCES OF DISCOURAGEMENT

Parenting supervisors must understand the sources of discouragement in young people to understand how to help them come out of the discouragement. "How they were raised!" is the curt answer given so often. This is partially true. Children often live in families that are unhealthy, even demoralizing, and sometimes destructive to their sense of worth. These children may be typically abused, if not according to the usual definitions of "abuse", at least by the standards of effective child care training. Sometimes the discouraged child is overly disciplined, or not disciplined at all. In either case, the child comes to believe he or she is worthless.

In *Reclaiming Youth at Risk* (Brendtro, Brokenleg, Van Brockern, National Educational Service, 1990) focused on the four seeds of discouragement experienced by youth at risk. They noted how these "seeds" resulted in tragedy for the youth in Native American families by causing them to be discouraged.

"Consider these children to have fallen among thieves, the thieves of ignorance and sin and ill fate and loss. Their birthrights were stolen. They have no belongings." (Karl Menninger, as quoted in Reclaiming Youth at Risk, pg. 8)

These perceptive authors describe four of the causes of discouragement:

1) Destructive Relationships (hungry for love)

2) Climates of Futility (feelings of inadequacy)
3) Learned Irresponsibility (powerlessness)
4) Loss of Purpose (self-centered)

These four sources, or "climates" of discouragement will be examined in the following paragraphs. We would add a fifth source of discouragement, namely,

5) The failure of their family parenting system resulted in a sense of betrayal.

Such children "at risk", can be reclaimed by competent parenting supervisors who re-instill courage, or personal confidence in the discouraged child. In *Reclaiming Youth at Risk* the authors describe a "Circle of Courage" that brings them back to confident independence.

The process they propose involves the following changes in the child's self-concept:

Belonging:

Restoring a healthy sense of attachment in the child. One of the major emotional traumas of youth who are at risk is that they have become disconnected from significant people and behaviors.

Mastery:

Acquiring a sense of confidence and personal success is essential for the self-identity of a child. Achieving and mastering *something* is built into our persona. Youth at risk often master the wrong things.

Independence:

The feeling of being individually responsible is crucial for a young person struggling with issues. The catch-twenty-two is that the very thing that child craves is the same thing that keeps him or her enslaved in dependency, rather than independence.

Generosity:

A benevolent attitude toward others is one of the strongest motivation for personal improvement. Young people must learn the biblical lesson that "it is more blessed to give than to receive."

In professional child care we have used the term, "troubled child" to describe a discouraged young person. Usually we are talking about our own attitudes toward them rather than the child's actual mental state. These discouraged children are troubled, but we may contribute to their pain by the way we label them. How often have your heard "at risk" children referred to in the following ways?

> We don't have that here/We can't do that here
> We are tired of dealing with him/her
> This will not fit in my schedule
> He/she doesn't care
> He/she is bi-polar
> Day One, I knew he/she didn't belong here
> He/she belongs somewhere else
> Somewhere else will make a difference
> I can't sacrifice the safety of other students
> I need to set an example for others
> He/she just has no morals

These statements may help us make sense of our world, but they may also be detrimental to our ability to really understand a discouraged child. Parenting supervisors must help youth find solutions to their problems, not add to them with labels and tags. How we view troubled children, and what labels we attach to their misbehaviors, may limit our abilities to help them.

There are some specific situations that seem to foster children at risk. These are described as climates to help us understand discouragement in the larger social world that produces "children at risk."

CLIMATES OF DISCOURAGEMENT

Think of the process of discipline as we study the "climates of discouragement" that produce the environments so detrimental to youth. Think of the problem, or crisis situation that demanded the discipline. Think of the big picture that the child found themselves in which produced the cause of the discipline, the child's *world*. In other words, what in that child's life brought him or her to *that?* Try to see what they saw in *their world!*

The five sources, or climates, of discouragement that follow will define the environments, or global situations, that are conducive to discouragement. (Taken from *Reclaiming Youth at Risk")*

1 – DESTRUCTIVE RELATIONSHIPS:

Destructive relationships are the first climate conducive to discouragement for a child. Brendtro *et al* write about a discouraged seventeen-year-old young man. He described himself as an "outcast" and was very lonely with many attempts at suicide. Once he was found sitting outside a convenience store bleeding at both wrists. Another time he was found inside a dog house with "please help me" written on the wall with his own blood. Finally, Richard Cardinal, age 17, hanged himself from a board suspended between two birch trees at his last foster home. (*Reclaiming Youth at Risk,* pg. 9).

This young man's world made him feel all alone. He felt that the only way to solve his problem was to end his life. He was not attached, or bonded, with anyone. His social world did not support him, but to the contrary, contributed to his decision. This is an illustration of a child who has *no one* to support him . . . at least, as he saw it!

Notice some of the characteristics of social group effect on those who *belong* and those who *do not belong.* These words describe a child who does not feel like he or she belongs:

Guarded
Rejected
Lonely
Promiscuous
Aloof
Isolated
Distrustful
Gang loyalty

When a child feels like he or she does not in fit, or belong, that child begins to overcompensate by *proving* that they *do belong!* In these cases, if they can't be the "best of the best", they become the "best of the worst"!

JOY: A CASE STUDY

The second illustration that follows concerns a young girl named "Joy". There were many people in this young girl's social life, but most of them were destructive. This case study was presented to professionals at a state child care conference in Georgia. "Joy" is not her real name, but the story is real.

Put yourself in "Joy's" shoes as you consider her relationships. Try to feel what she felt when the significant parental supervisors around her were destructive to her character? The case of "Joy" is real. Look closely at her story. Particularly notice her relationships with others. Most of her relationships were destructive to her self-esteem and contributed to her sense of worthlessness. Notice how the destructive relationships she experienced nearly became deadly! Note also the typical way supervising adults dealt with

Joy. As a parenting supervisor you must be able to honestly say, *"I feel your pain!"*

─────

JOY!? WHERE'S THE JOY.

(Actual case, but names and dates changed)
DOB: 08-11-78
JOY M. is a 16-year-old white female
JOY appears to be healthy and smart. She can perform at the "A" level in school, but has been diagnosed as "Manic Depressive" and is taking Lithium. Verbal IQ of 116, performance IQ 115, and composite IQ 116.

Study carefully the relationships in her life:
- Bob, her biological father
- Kathy, her biological mother
- Sammy, her sister
- Jimmy, her stepfather
- Foster parents #1#2#3#4#5#6#7#8#9
- Foster parents #10#11#12#13#14
- #15 – Last placement – residential program
- Her Best Friend
- Her Drug Dealer

JOY's father is BOB...no contact since Joy was 4 yrs. Old

JOY's mother is KATHY...moved to Kansas in 1990.

JOY has a younger sister, SAMMY, who is two years younger. She is now in a troubled children's center.

JOY's mother divorced her stepfather JIMMY.

JOY has been in FOSTER CARE #1 in ___ County while her mother was in a mental hospital in 1984.

JOY's mother took an overdose in 1984 when she learned that Jimmy has sexually abused the girls.

JOY was then moved to another FOSTER HOME #2 in ____ County.

JOY has attempted suicide five times between 1984 and 1991.

JOY was sexually provocative.

JOY was sexually abused by her natural father BOB.

JOY was sexually abused by her stepfather JIMMY.

JOY was sexually abused by a foster father.

JOY has failed placements in nine (9) counties.

JOY's BEST FRIEND committed suicide.

JOY's friends at "the Home" call her a "lesbian" and will not have anything to do with her.

JOY claims she was beaten up by her DRUG DEALER, but, her teacher said she personally observed Joy injuring herself.

JOY claims she is tense all the time...has nightmares at night

JOY says no one likes her.

Look closely at the way Joy's relationships developed and changed, you will notice that in the end the only relationship that seemed to stand the test of time was with *her drug dealer!*

Notice how the destructive relationships in Joy's world led to *separation, isolation and alienation.* When a child's world is predominately negative toward them, that child begins to lose heart, and becomes discouraged.

What are some tips for parenting supervisors in such situations? First, understand that in both the case of Richard and Joy they did not have a sense of belonging. Encourage such children to become members of good social groups. Help them form coalitions with others to make good friends. Take the time to be a "friend", as well as a supervisor. Help them become a team player!

2 – CLIMATES OF HOSTILITY

The second environment that produces discouragement could be described as a climate of hostility.

In this world a child feels that everyone, including the parenting supervisors, are against them. They think the rules of the family treat them unfairly, or were made just for them. These children can learn what is expected of them, but they do not think they can measure up! Their world is a hostile place to live, with threats and enemies everywhere!

Negative and demeaning family relationships produce young people who ask, "What's the use of trying"! Labeling a child "deviant, or delinquent" may create an environment of futility. Not only is this world hostile, but it is also futile for them to even try.

What is missing in this world is a sense of achievement. Failure seems to be the rule. The discouraged child would fall under the "failure" label: non-achiever, failure-oriented, avoidance of risks, fears challenge, unmotivated, gives in easily, feels inadequate.

Conversely, a successful child may be described as: focuses on strengths, has successful experiences, is creative, a problem-solver, motivated to act, persistent, and competent.

A son worked nights in a Pizza parlor. One night he was stopped by police after midnight when coming home from his job because the tag on the car had not been changed. Arrested, he was taken to the police station and his parents were called. The parents went to the station in the early morning hours to pick him up. On the way home he was most disturbed because he heard the police say,

"I have a juvenile driving without a car tag."

"Dad, he called me a juvenile!"
(He thought juvenile-delinquent!)

This climate of hostility may be telegraphed to the child with daily put-down communications! The messages they hear are: "You can't do anything right!" or, "You made your bed, now sleep in it!", "____are just a bad egg!", "You won't amount to anything!" When children hear these things from their most significant others, these children become discouraged thinking they just can't do anything right!

One translation of Colossians 3:21 states that a child may just "quit trying" when the child becomes discouraged:

Fathers, don't aggravate your children. If you do, they will become discouraged and quit trying. (Colossians 3:21: New Living Translation)

⚜

CASE STUDY: ALLEN: "WHAT DO YOU CARE?"

Allen was a marginal student who barely made his grades. He had to have lots of help. We had arranged for a private tutor to give him extra help. Yet, he had missed his tutoring class again, for the 'nth time! I found him on the playground... just swinging!

I sat down in a swing next to his, and began arguing the case that he needed tutoring...and that his grades had to be passing...and that if he did not graduate from high school he would not get a good job...and that ...but he abruptly stopped me with:

"WHAT DO YOU CARE!? My mother does not care! My sister doesn't care! *WHAT DO YOU CARE?"*

Allen felt all alone, with no real attachments. His mother had missed her "visitation" meeting again! She just didn't show up.

Allen was looking down a long dark tunnel that seemed to go nowhere! It began in his natural home, but seemed to continue in his foster placement. He did not see any light at the end of the tunnel! Allen was in a world of hostile futility. He needed to be successful at something. He needed to have others around him (like his mother) who would give him a sense of worth.

A discouraged child can find strength and power from personal achievement. Going to school, making the grades and being a part of a winning team... these things give a child the sense of worth and competence.

3 – LEARNED HELPLESSNESS

The third climate or environment conducive to discouragement is learned helplessness that results in irresponsibility. These children are not only detached from good relationships, but they do not feel responsible, or accountable for their conduct. They are quick to blame others. A discouraged child feels helpless, because that is what they have learned from their earlier experiences.

The goal of a parenting supervisor, as stated earlier, is to supervise a dependent child to become an independent adult. This goal focuses on the task of becoming autonomous, self-sufficient. Other words that describe this goal are: confident, assertive, responsible, inner-control, self-disciplined, and leaders. These terms describe an independently acting person.

The opposite words describe the discouraged child who believes that they are helpless, when they are not! They are: dependent, passive, lacks self-esteem, feels inferior, manipulative, rebellious, defiant, and engages in power struggles.

Children in our care have often been trained by adults with poor parenting skills. There are indicators telling us that the child learned helplessness, defiant rebellion against authority, self-serving narcissism, and negative peer relations from the parents, or the lack of parents!

Their "training" could be described as almost total freedom with no restrictions. These children lived in self-indulgence having every desire either fulfilled or ignored. The climate of their world was survival-motivated for both the adults and the children. They experienced a training loss, or void, which is a loss of internalized MORAL VALUES! Many, even in the poorest families, when given whatever they wanted, felt entitled. The only value was a selfish drive to survive.

Darrel, 14 years old, came to "the home" with his two sisters because his mother (a single parent) just did not stay home and care for the children. Darrel was afraid his sisters could not make it living in the girl's cottage since they had relied on their big brother for years.

Actually, Darrel nearly did not make it! Why? Because he had been given everything he wanted by his absent mother: freedom to do what he wanted, when he wanted and how he wanted! He was a fourteen-year-old in charge!

Excessive permissiveness (sometimes granted by the absence of the parent) results in a child becoming *a young tyrant.* Some parents are not so much "permissive" as they are *INDIFFERENT.* They just don't take time to care...too busy with their own problems and lives!

These children, raised in a care-*less* parenting fashion, are often deviant. They develop a strong resistance to affection, conscience, and "what's right and wrong". The issue is one of learned helplessness resulting in *learned irresponsibility.* What is lacking is a sense of personal independence, or autonomy.

4 – LOSS OF PURPOSE, OR DIRECTION

The fourth climate of discouragement describes youth who have lost their way with no purpose in life. One of the causes for this is the indulgence noted earlier. Such youth did not develop the relationships of life that would allow them to go outside themselves. This discouraged youth would be self-centered, selfish, and aggressive (Brendtro, *et al).* Terms to describe this environment are: selfish, affectionless, narcissistic, co-dependent, aloof, antisocial, and bullies' others. They feel that they are going *nowhere* and they want to make sure others go with them! The discouraged child has lost his or her way!

Two psychologists at Duke University speak of how "selfishness" has contributed to this destructive lost-*ness:*

"There is currently in our society an enormous emphasis on the self...narcissism, self-concern and preoccupation with "me" ...human behavior is reduced to the pursuit of selfishness"

Our ability to reach out to others and to consider the values of our society depends on how successfully we internalized the moral values of that society. Indulgent children tend to be self-serving, narcissistic sociopaths who are seemingly incapable of concern for others.

The Bible teaches us to be generous...to be givers! We often quote that it is *"more blessed to give than to receive"*, but most of us like to receive! Children under our care may be selfish and self-serving, to the point, possibly, of petty theft for what they want. Many times they have violated the social standards with impunity!

In a child sexual abuse case it was reported that the parents actually "trained" a child to do sex acts with them. From an early age they would laugh at his sexual antics. (Any wonder that he became a sexual perpetrator!)

We must teach children to accept purposes larger than themselves, and to sacrificially give toward those goals! This true story from the holocaust about the family of Solomon Rosenberg and his family sadly illustrates the value of purpose, commitment and direction:

Solomon Rosenberg and his wife, two sons, and his mother and father were arrested and placed in a concentration camp. A Nazi labor camp! Simple rules: 'AS LONG AS YOU CAN DO YOUR WORK, YOU ARE PERMITTED TO LIVE. WHEN YOU BECOME TOO WEAK TO DO YOUR WORK, THEN YOU ARE EXTERMINATED."

Rosenberg watched his mother and his father marched off to their deaths, and he knew that next would be his youngest Son, David, because David was a frail child unable to work.

Every evening Rosenberg came back into the barracks after his hours of labor and searched for the faces of his family. When he found them they would huddle together, embrace one another, and thank God for another day of life.

One day Rosenberg came back and didn't see those familiar faces. He finally discovered his oldest son, Joshua, in a corner, huddled, weeping, and praying.

"Josh, tell me it's not true".
Joshua turned and said, "It is true, Poppa. Today David was not strong enough to do his work. So they came for him."

"But where is your mother?" Asked Mr. Rosenberg.

"Oh, Poppa," he said, "When they came for David he was afraid and cried.

Momma said, "There is nothing to be afraid of, David, and she took his hand and went with him."

Think about this story and how it illustrates the four points of the Circle of Courage. How do we, as parenting supervisors help a discouraged child gain courage?   The words that define that need are:
- generosity,
- caring for others,
- sharing what we have with others,
- loyal to a cause,
- the ability to feel with others and
- generally supportive of others.

5 – FAILURE OF THEIR FAMILY PARENTING SYSTEM

The fifth cause, or climate conducive to discouraging a child is a *perceived,* or *real* failure of their family parenting system. These children feel betrayed. Either their parenting supervisors were not trained adequately, or they were not properly motivated to supervise the development of strong character. Their actual conduct may not have been congruent with their stated values, or was poorly managed. The family system may not have provided the help a child needed to survive in the modern world.

We often define these families as "dysfunctional." Sometimes we blame the generation gap, or the bad-old-world out there! The discouraged child just feels betrayed and over time, migrates to, what to him or her, is a *safer* world. That may be a deviant street gang, or worse!

Parenting supervisors must understand that discouraging a child is the major risk they face when administering discipline. That is one of the key reasons many of the consequences involved in effective discipline in the ABC system are pre-planned and pre-prescribed. Discipline should only be administered when the parenting supervisors are emotionally stable and under control.

Abuse is the second danger to a child during discipline. An outline description will at least introduce the subject for discussion.

Discussion Question:

1) What are the three (3) purposes for disciplining a child?

2) Define "discouragement".

3) Why is "discouragement" a danger?

4) List the five climates suggested that are conducive to discouragement.

5) List five words that describe a discouraged youth according to this study.

6) Why would "fathers" need to be told to not provoke a child to anger?

7) How does the story of "Joy" illustrate destructive relationships?

8) Explain the impact of negative, always demeaning communication upon a child.

9) What is narcissism? Why is it destructive?

10) Explain why teaching a child to be generous is good.

11) How does purpose and commitment to a larger cause inspire independence?

12) Define courage and discourage.

Chapter 9

⚜

DANGER: Child Abuse

PARENTING SUPERVISION PRINCIPLES

30 *Parenting supervisors must know the difference in corrective discipline and child abuse.*

31 *Recognizing the symptoms of child abuse is important in effective parenting.*

IMPORTANT WARNING

Effective parenting comes with the pressures of corrective discipline. Anyone who assumes the very important role of training children must include correcting them when they violate the code of conduct established. Disobedience is a failure on the part of the child to meet the standards, but it may be viewed by the parenting supervisors as a challenge to their authority. Discipline, by its very nature involves emotional responses. It is not unusual for an adult to feel emotionally angry with a child's disobedience. Therein lies the danger and the possibility of the parents abusing the child. Child abuse is a real threat in effective child care supervision.
****

In the state of Georgia there are more than twenty thousand (20,000) children in "out-of-home" care. More than 14,000 of these are under the care of private, mostly faith-based, agencies. Hundreds more are still living at home, but are directly under the care of the Department of Human Services due to family hardships, history of child abuse/neglect, or other environmental circumstances that identify these children "at risk". Most of these children are in foster care, residential foster care, or living in their own homes under the supervision of DFAC workers.

A study of the children coming into "out-of-home" care who have been reared in dysfunctional families will help us understand the merits of effective parenting. These children were sometimes victims. Abuse is commonly reported by children who come from such dysfunctional families! These abused children typically experience more problems than children from healthy families.

Effective parenting skills must include the ability to identify and avoid child abuse. It is possible for good parents to legally abuse a child! Professionals should be able to quickly identify the children of abuse. This chapter will present a very sketchy outline of the most common forms of legal child abuse with identifying symptoms. All parenting supervisors would do well to do additional study on this topic.

THE RISK OF CHILD ABUSE

The typical young person who is "at risk" coming into care at Raintree Village is between the ages of 13-15, and more often than not, has behavioral, and/or emotional problems. Most of them are victims of neglect, abandonment, or abuse. A more clearly defined child in care (*The example of "Joy"*) demonstrates how the victimization cycle continues. The incidence of abuse in our society is the source of most of the placements and problems we face in our work in residential child care.

By definition according to Georgia law, child abuse is:

- Physical injury or death inflicted upon a child by a parent or caretaker thereof, by other than accidental means; provided, however, physical forms of discipline may be used as long as there is not physical injury to the child;

- Neglect or exploitation of a child by a parent of caretaker thereof;

- Sexual abuse or sexual exploitation of a child.

- No child, who in good faith is being treated solely by spiritual means through prayer in accordance with the tenets and practices of a recognized church or religious denomination by a duly accredited practitioner thereof shall, for that reason alone, be considered to be an "abused" child.

In most U.S. states, the legal definition of child molestation is: an act of a person, adult, or child, who forces, coerces, or threatens a child to have any form of sexual contact, or to engage in any type of sexual activity at the perpetrator's direction.

Sexual abuse shall not include consensual sex acts involving persons of the opposite sex when the sex acts are between minors or between a minor and an adult who is not more than five years older than the minor. This provision shall not be deemed or constructed to repeal any law concerning the age of capacity to consent.

The Department of Family and Children Services must immediately notify the appropriate police authority or district attorney of reports containing any allegation or evidence of child abuse.

[Source: "Child Abuse & Neglect Reporting Law," Georgia Code Section 19-7-5 and National Child Abuse and Neglect Data System (NCANDS)-Project of the National Center of Child Abuse and Neglect (NCCAN): US Department of Health and Human Services, 1997.]

The statues are different from state-to-state to legally define child abuse. The point is clear: *Child abuse is a crime in every state.* Professional parenting supervisors are especially at risk.

NATIONALLY, THE VICTIMS OF CHILD ABUSE

An estimated 896,000 children were determined to be victims of child abuse or neglect for 2002. The rate of victimization per 1,000 children in the national population has dropped from 13.4 children in 1990 to 12.3 children in 2002.

WHAT TYPES OF MALTREATMENT WERE FOUND?

More than 60 percent of child victims were *neglected* by their parents or other caregivers. Almost 20 percent were *physically abused*, 10 percent were *sexually abused*, and 7 percent were *emotionally maltreated*. In addition, almost 20 percent were associated with "other" types of maltreatment based on specific State laws and policies. A child could be a victim of more than one type of maltreatment.

WHAT WERE THE CHARACTERISTICS OF VICTIMS?
- Children ages birth to 3 years had the highest rates of victimization at 16.0 per 1,000 children.
- Girls were slightly more likely to be victims than boys.
- American Indian or Alaska Native and African-American children had the highest rates of victimization when compared to their national population.
- While the rate of White victims of child abuse or neglect was 10.7 per 1,000 children of the same

race, the rate for American Indian or Alaska Natives was 21.7 per 1,000 children and for African-Americans 20.2 per 1,000 children.

STATISTICS FOR GEORGIA . . .

- In 2002, there were nearly 85,464 reports of child abuse and neglect.
- Every 30 minutes a child in Georgia is the victim of confirmed abuse or neglect.
- It costs only $3 per year per child to teach violence prevention in schools.
- It costs about $36,000 a year to house a child in a Georgia youth detention center.

Thus, the real malady in poor parenting is abuse! Parents abuse the authority given to them by their Creator, and violate their parental responsibilities by sexually, physically, and emotionally abusing those under their supervision, their children!

INDICATORS OF CHILD ABUSE

Every professional supervising children needs to know what child abuse is, and how to recognize it in the children in their care. Not only is it illegal, but it is the prime source of discouragement in a child. In addition, child abuse is the basic threat in the use of parental authority.

Therefore, we need to briefly review child abuse to maintain proper and appropriate standards, especially during crisis situations requiring that corrective discipline be applied.

SEXUAL ABUSE

This abuse occurs when an adult or older child exploits a child for sexual gratification. Sexual abuse includes fondling, sodomy, child prostitution, incest, and encouraging or forcing a child to participate in pornographic activities.

Some of the physical Indicators of this are:
> difficulty in walking or sitting
> torn, stained or bloody underclothing
> pain, swelling or itching in genital area
> pain upon urination
> bruises, bleeding or laceration in external genitals, vaginal/anal areas
> vaginal/penile discharge
> venereal disease
> poor sphincter tone
> excessive masturbation

Some behavioral Indicators are:
> unwilling to change for gym or participate in PE classes
> withdrawal, fantasy or infantile behavior
> bizarre, sophisticated or unusual sexual behavior or knowledge
> poor peer relationships
> delinquent or runaway
> reports sexual assaults by caretaker
> change in performance in school
> sleeping disorders/nightmares
> eating disorders
> aggressive acting out
> self-abusive behaviors: drug addictions, alcohol addiction, self-mutilation
> sexual acting-out on younger children

PHYSICAL ABUSE:

Physical abuse occurs when a child suffers a non-accidental injury that may include severe beatings, burns, fractures, bruises, welts, or other physical problems.

Some physical abuse Indicators are:
- ➤ Unexplained bruises and welts on face, lips, mouth, or on torso, back, buttocks, thighs in various stages of healing
- ➤ Clustered injuries, forming regular patterns (e.g., electrical cord, belt) on several different surface areas
- ➤ Injuries that regularly appear after absence, weekend, or vacation
- ➤ Unexplained fractures/dislocations to skull, nose, facial structure in various stages of healing
- ➤ multiple or spinal fracture
- ➤ Unexplained burns cigar, cigarette burns, especially on soles, palms, backs, or buttocks
- ➤ immersion burns (sock-like, glove-like, doughnut-shaped on buttocks or genitals)
- ➤ infected burns, indicating delay in seeking treatment
- ➤ Bald patches on the scalp

Some behavioral Indicators of physical abuse are:
- ➤ feels deserving of punishment
- ➤ wary of adult contact
- ➤ apprehensive when others cry
- ➤ behavioral extremes: aggressiveness or withdrawal
- ➤ frightened of parents
- ➤ afraid to go home
- ➤ reports injury by parent
- ➤ vacant or frozen stare
- ➤ lies very still while surveying surroundings
- ➤ responds to questions in monosyllables
- ➤ inappropriate or precocious maturity

- ➤ manipulative behavior to get attention,
- ➤ capable of only superficial relationships
- ➤ indiscriminately seeks affection
- ➤ poor self-concept

EMOTIONAL ABUSE:

Emotional abuse is more difficult to prove. It occurs when a parent creates a negative emotional atmosphere for the child. Examples are when the parent makes continued unfavorable comparisons to a sibling, when the parent makes the child feel bad because he or she is not perfect, or when the parent uses shameful forms of punishment.

Some physical Indicators of emotional abuse are:
- ➤ speech disorders
- ➤ lags in physical development
- ➤ failure to thrive
- ➤ hyperactive/disruptive behavior

Some behavioral Indicators for emotional abuse are:
- ➤ habit disorders (sucking, biting, rocking, etc.)
- ➤ conduct/learning disorders
- ➤ neurotic traits (sleep disorders, inhibition of play, unusual fearfulness)
- ➤ psychoneurotic reactions (hysteria, obsessions, compulsions, phobias, hypochondriasis)
- ➤ behavior extremes
- ➤ overly adaptive behaviors
- ➤ suicide attempts
- ➤ developmental lags

NEGLECT:

Neglect occurs when a parent or caretaker allows a child to experience avoidable suffering or fails to provide basic essentials for physical, social, and emotional development. Although it is passive, rather than active abuse, it is nonetheless, abuse.

Some physical Indicators of neglect are:
- underweight, poor growth patterns, failure to thrive
- consistent hunger, poor hygiene, inappropriate dress
- consistent lack of supervision, especially in dangerous activities or for long periods of time
- wasting of subcutaneous tissue
- unattended physical problems or medical needs
- abandonment
- bald patches on the scalp

Some behavioral Indicators of neglect are:
- begging, stealing food
- extended stays at school (early arrival and late departure)
- rare attendance at school
- constant fatigue, listlessness or falling asleep in class
- inappropriate seeking of affection
- assuming adult responsibilities and concerns
- alcohol or drug abuse
- delinquency
- reports that there is no caretaker

AVOIDING CHILD ABUSE

The ABC system was developed in the late 1980's at a time when the threat of child abuse by professional parenting supervisors became news. Not only was our world becoming more violent, but more and more professionals were being charged with abuse. Some major innovative programs, such as out-bound wilderness programs, were being closed down and their leaders charged with abuse. More than a few direct care supervisors were either charged or lost their jobs because of abuse allegations.

The purpose of this study is not to determine the guilt or innocence in such cases where abuse has been alleged. Suffice it to say, child abuse is wrong. Both natural parents and professional supervisors of children should stand should-to-shoulder to avoid it and expose it.

There some things we can do to avoid abusing our children and in identifying when children are abused:

1. Use every opportunity to learn how to be an effective parenting supervisor. Read good books. Go to informational websites such as the Child Welfare League of America.

2. Administer discipline, especially corrective discipline, carefully with a cool head. Never discipline when your emotions are raging. It takes time to raise a child...think about it over night!

3. Communicate with your children, especially if you are a professional supervisor, to identify signs of abuse. Others may be abusing, but you have the duty to stop it.

Discussion Questions:

1) Why are corrective discipline and child abuse related?

2) Explain why more abuse is reported in dysfunctional families?

3) Legally, define "child abuse" for your state? How might this differ from other states' laws on child abuse?

4) Do the ages of the child and his/her abuser make a difference?

Chapter 10

⟨❦⟩

CHANGE:
A Lifetime Challenge

PARENTING SUPERVISION PRINCIPLES

32 Character to last a lifetime must be strong, but flexible.

33 Effective parenting prepares and controls for difficult circumstances.

34 Character can become stronger under adversity.

The title of this chapter should not be construed to mean that the formation of character ends when a person becomes an adult. To the contrary, a person's character continues to evolve over the years through the same process that is suggested earlier ... *good choices chained together to result in responsible behaviors!* The *process framework* for making good decisions should continue for a lifetime. Our decision-experiences are the components that form good character. *Good* character changes over time when good choices result in better good character. The converse is also true; a person can chain together bad choices that effectively change the framework of character.

However, it is true that parenting supervisors are the major players in training children to develop character.

As the previous chapters have outlined, most of the heavy lifting is done in monitoring and correcting the small simple routine every day choices as a child. Effective parenting supervisors carefully direct and discipline children to make acceptable choices. The process of organizing those choices and subsequent behaviors result a decision-making framework we call *character*. Supervising the formation of character in children is arguably the most important thing one generation can do for the next. In the first chapter you were reminded of the Scripture that says:

> *"Children, obey your parents in the Lord, for this is right. "Honor your father and mother"—which is the first commandment with a promise— "so that it may go well with you and that you may enjoy long life on the earth."* (Ephesians 6:1-3 NIV).

This passage indicates that the work you do can last a lifetime! In fact, it affirms that when a child learns *how* to submit to the authority of the parenting supervisors, and imbibe values that are conveyed, that child will live a long enjoyable life. Essentially, this means a well-developed character based on valid standards of conduct and buffeted by adversity, can *thrive* in any life circumstance. The tools for survival are securely placed in a person's toolbox of character.

This chapter is more a bonus, or reward, than basic instruction in forming character. Parenting supervisors *really* should probably have read this chapter first, rather than now! Next, we will suggest what the *finished* product of character should look like. Then, the perfect model described in the Epilogue is the cherry on top! Parenting supervision is a wonderfully rewarding responsibility...*with adversities!*

CHARACTER TO SURVIVE THE STORMS

Ever since the first skyscraper was built in Chicago in 1885 engineers and architects have had to deal with the problem of wind stress, or "wind loading". Tall buildings must be built to sway with the pressures of wind. Guests at the Grand Hyatt in San Francisco are given notes at check-in informing them that the building will creak as it sways. At 2,717 feet, the Burj Khalifa, formerly known as the Burj Dubai, sways more than six feet at the very top! Swaying allows the building to flex with the pressures without breaking.

Forming character in a child is much like building a skyscraper to withstand the stress of wind. Like bamboo in a hurricane, solid character will bend, but not break! Our lives are grounded by the framework of character that hold everything in place making it possible to stand against the storms of life. The management of this stress becomes the basic function of our character.

Throughout this study we have referred to "character" more as a process, or the organizing framework for decision-making, rather than a just a constellation of traits. When a child develops a strong character that child can make wise choices and become a stable member of society. The resilient part of character is the ability to organize and prioritize our routine experiences and daily behaviors and make acceptable decisions. At first, the basic values that certify the acceptable choices we make are the values of our parenting supervisors. These values are communicated to us by basic instruction, modeling example, and corrective discipline. Later, as we grow more experienced, good character can confidently challenge their contemporary world and become the guide to changes for the future. Character and change go together. Solid character not only supports us during times of challenge, but it also enables us to change with the times.

Significant relationships, particularly the child/ parenting supervisor relationship, are crucial in the child's character development. Teachers, coaches, "bosses", friends, and even enemies play a major role in forming a child's character. A child's behaviors are constantly monitored, supervised, and reported back to the child as "acceptable" or "unacceptable" ...a *plus* or a *minus,* by these significant others. This pattern of these recurrent experiences, chained together, subsequently shape the character of the child. A child will not develop a healthy character if that child feels ignored, rejected, invalidated, devalued, shamed, or punished by the "significant others", especially the parenting supervisors. This inner self-control framework allows our world to "sway" without breaking. That's the goal we all seek in successfully parenting a child.

CHANGE IN OUR WORLD

Change *is* a part of our world. How a child learns to manage change is critical for successful functioning as an adult. Our world is changing at a rapid rate. Alvin Toffler (1970) made a detailed study of the acceleration of change and its psychological effects. He suggested that it would lead to a set of severe physical and mental disturbances, which he called the "future shock" syndrome.

Technology changes of the past fifty years have literally revolutionized our lives. Change, and coping with the stress associated with it, is a major challenge for any person. What worked for us in the past may seem to be less effective today. This may include our values and standards as well. Change shocks our sense of stability and can cause us to question everything, including the basic values framing our character.

The ABC system for character formation addresses the components of change. In fact, the ten Levels are designed to help a child *change* for the better by moving up in the system. Over time a child will learn that change can be good, but frightening. The rewards and privileges associated with the ascending levels can stabilize a child's life into a pattern of decision-making that results in personal peace. The fact is, one risk of *the process* is that a child may become smug, snobbish, and even rigid in "the system". In professional child care we call this "institutionalization". These children have learned to "work the system" for the worse, not the better! They have become comfortable in their present stage of life and do not want to change. In the adult world we may tag this trait with the label "traditional".

On the other hand, parenting supervisors are taught to use the components of change to modify, or change the behaviors of children. In the ABC system the components for change are: *rewards, restriction, communications* and *time.* Parenting supervisors manipulate these four components to train the decision-making process of character formation. The daily routines of personal care, family duties and routine community responsibilities are used to help a child in coping with change. A child's self-confidence gets stronger by successfully stringing positive experiences together over time. These experiences of acceptable choices are rewarded by the significant others in the child's life. Rewards could be anything from just saying "good job" simply stated, or, a pat on the back or additional spending money. The point is, we change when we get something we like, or need, or enjoy doing. One person's "reward" may not be the same as it is for another. Negative painful consequences from bad choices are typically avoided.

ADVERSITY

The ABC system process described throughout this study is a training process in learning how to live in a world of "change". Getting use to the "good changes", like promotions to a better life or other opportunities of joy is easy. But, when the storms of life come, that is a different story! Someone has said we should train a child to be a 35-year old adult living in the real world. Some would argue that adversity builds character. It is reported that Eleanor Roosevelt believed we should "do one thing every day that scares" us. Ralph Waldo Emerson said it like this, "Do the thing you fear, and the death of fear is certain".

The implications are clear: every person is challenged to change, and grow. You cannot get stronger without exercising in the real world. The real world is a world of trial and adversity. It comes in many forms including serious sickness, financial crisis, personal loss, divorce, death and natural disasters. Effective parenting prepares a child to enjoy living in the real world.

RESILIENCE

Even the Scriptures talk about the pain of having your faith tested by trials. (James 1:2-3). They indicate that the ability to endure, or persevere, is produced by the testing. This is another way of saying your inner framework of character is challenged by adversity, but can grow stronger. Effective parenting supervisors want the children they train to be strong, to not just to survive in the storms of life, but to thrive! The term that describes this trait is "resilience" which is, the capacity to rise above difficult circumstances and continue to exist in this less-than-perfect world. Hara Estroff Marano said "at the heart of resilience is a belief in oneself –yet also a belief in something larger than oneself" (*Psychology Today*, The Art of Resilience). Resilience is the process of adjusting or coping with trauma and then bouncing back. Such recovery is a common characteristic of people with strong guiding characters.

Grit is another term used to describe this ability of the inner framework of a person to withstand negative circumstances. True grit is innate with the values of the character. Like the grit on a grindstone, these values manage the resistance of tough times with stability and balance to smooth things out.

CHARACTER FOR A LIFETIME

So, in times of trouble, adults well-trained by effective parenting while young, are capable of fortifying their confidence and maintaining their balance even under challenge. Instead of being pulled under by the torrents, they ride the waves of adversity. How? Why do some master the art of resilience and others literally fall apart?

Two important things for a parenting supervisor are: a) knowing what makes a strong character, and b) knowing how to best supervise its formation in a child. These are the capstones of character development. Numerous writers and dozens of lists of traits can be found that instruct on building character strength in young people.

Dr. Kenneth Ginsburg is a pediatrician specializing in Adolescent Medicine at The Children's Hospital of Philadelphia and a Professor of Pediatrics at the University of Pennsylvania School of Medicine. He has developed "The 7 Cs: The Essential Building Blocks of Resilience" (www.FosteringResilience) to outline the target goals (tags) for resilience in children and teens.

Listed below are Ginsberg's outline for building resilience in young people. More details and contemporary information may be found on the website.

Bottom Line #1: *"Young people live up or down to expectations we set for them. They need adults who believe in them unconditionally and hold them to the high expectations of being compassionate, generous, and creative.*

Competence:

When we notice what young people are doing right and give them opportunities to develop important skills, they feel competent. We undermine competence when we don't allow young people to recover themselves after a fall.

Confidence:

Young people need confidence to be able to navigate the world, think outside the box, and recover from challenges.

Connection:

Connections with other people, schools, and communities offer young people the security that allows them to stand on their own and develop creative solutions.

Character:

Young people need a clear sense of right and wrong and a commitment to integrity.

Contribution:

Young people who contribute to the well-being of others will receive gratitude rather than condemnation. They will learn that contributing feels good and may therefore more easily turn to others, and do so without shame.

Coping:

Young people who possess a variety of healthy coping strategies will be less likely to turn to dangerous quick fixes when stressed.

Control:

Young people who understand privileges and respect are earned through demonstrated responsibility will learn to make wise choices and feel a sense of control.

Bottom Line #2: *What we do to model healthy resilience strategies for our children is more important than anything we say about them".*

Brad Waters ("Cultivating Resilience for Total Well-Being", <u>Design your Path,</u> May 21, 2013) listed ten traits of resilient people. These are characteristics they seem to possess:

1. *They know their boundaries.* Resilient people understand that there is a separation between who they are at their core and the cause of their *temporary* suffering.

2. *They keep good company.* Resilient people tend to seek out and surround themselves with other resilient people, whether just for fun or when there's a need for support.

3. *They cultivate self-awareness.* Being 'blissfully unaware' can get us through a bad day but it's not a very <u>wise</u> long-term strategy. The self-aware are good at listening to the subtle cues their body and their mood are sending.

4. *They practice acceptance.* Pain is painful, stress is stressful, and healing takes time. Resilient people understand that stress/pain is a part of living that ebbs and flows. Acceptance is not about giving up and letting the stress take over, it's about *leaning in* to experience the full range of emotions and trusting that we will bounce back.

5. *They're willing to sit in silence.* We all react differently to stress and trauma. Some of us shut down and some of us ramp up. Somewhere in the middle there is mindfulness -- being in the presence of the moment without judgment or avoidance.

6. *They don't have to have all the answers.* We can find strength in knowing that it's okay to not have

it all figured out right now and trusting that we will gradually find peace and *knowing* when our mind-body-soul is ready.

7. *They have a menu of self-care habits.* They have a mental list (perhaps even a physical list) of good habits that support them when they need it most.

8. *They enlist their team.* The most resilient among us know how to reach out for help. They know who will serve as a listening ear and, let's be honest, who won't! Our team of supporters helps us reflect back what they see when we're too immersed in overwhelm to witness our own coping.

9. *They consider the possibilities.* We can train ourselves to ask which parts of our current story are permanent and which can possibly change. *Can this situation be looked at in a different way that I haven't been considering?* This helps us maintain a realistic understanding that the present situation is being colored by our current interpretation. Our interpretations of our stories will always change as we grow and mature. Knowing that today's interpretation can and will change, gives us the faith and hope that things can feel better tomorrow.

10. *They get out of their head.* When we're in the midst of stress and overwhelmed, our thoughts can swirl with dizzying speed and disconnectedness. We can find reprieve by getting the thoughts out of our head and onto our paper.

Dr. Kenneth Ginsburg suggests a similar "to do" list for forming the capacity to thrive in a child during times of stress (Building Resilience in Children and Teens: Giving Kids Roots and Wings):

1. *Notice acts of kindness in your child.* Be sure to notice and praise children for their acts of kindness, generosity and thoughtfulness.

2. *Notice acts of kindness and decent behavior in others.* Let's begin talking to one another about positive things others do every day that go unnoticed. In other words, "Let's redefine our heroes and minimize our scandals and do it in front of kids." If we don't, we risk the chance of exposing children to a world much worse than it is, having an effect on how they view and interact in the world.

3. *Treat each other well.* Children are keenly aware of how adults treat each other. When treating each other with respect and patience children remember. When problems are discussed openly with thoughtfulness and resolved children learn it is okay to voice opinions and disagreements can be resolved respectfully.

4. *Treat strangers well.* Children learn character traits such as compassion through witnessing how you interact with others. No words can ever have as lasting impression on your child as the behavior you display.

5. *Reinforce the importance of including all children.* Instill confident values in your child by helping her realize the importance of other children's feelings, while still maintaining best friendships. Having a wide variety of friendships is a wonderful asset.

6. *Promote responsibility. Don't spoil your children.* Taking responsibility when things go wrong and then work to improve is a trait of resilient people. If taught to take responsibility for their actions, children will learn the cause and effect of good behavior and good works. Help children learn to be patient.

7. *Work towards a better world.* Volunteering is a wonderful service, maybe you don't have time to volunteer for several causes, but you have time to call a relative, pick up trash as you're walking by it, and open the door for the person behind you in the grocery store. It's the small things that collectively can make a difference too.

8. *Avoid Prejudice.* Prejudice can often be unconscious based on judgments made with limited information and preventing us from getting to know one another. Children will thrive in the world if they are raised in an environment free of bias. Expose children to positive messages of diverse groups.

9. *Believe in something bigger.* Whatever the something bigger may be. Something greater to turn to and the common connection with others can provide children with many character building lessons.

10. *Be human.* We are all human. Our challenge is to work so our better selves prevail over our unattractive, even destructive impulses.

Consider the following questions posed by Dr. Ginsburg to ponder how you contribute to the character development of your youth. (www.FosteringResilience)

Do I help my child understand how his behaviors affect other people in good and bad ways?

Am I helping my child recognize himself as a caring person?

Do I allow him to clarify his own values?

Do I allow him to consider right versus wrong and look beyond immediate satisfaction or selfish needs?

Do I value him so clearly that I model the importance of caring for others?

Do I demonstrate the importance of community?

Do I help him develop a sense of spirituality?

Am I careful to avoid racist, ethnic, or hateful statements or stereotypes?

Am I clear how I regard these thoughts and statements whenever and wherever my child is exposed to them?

Do I express how I think of others' needs when I make decisions or take actions?

HISTORY IN THE MAKING

Keep a daily journal of your parenting supervision. You are on an exciting journey with the children under your supervision. The experiences of that trip will be the very fiber of both your future and their past. You have been the most significant person of interest in this study, but the lives of the children you supervise will actually reflect the work you do. Write it down. Read what you write regularly, and later as adults, allow your charges to read it! You both will be blessed.

Regardless of the title of this book, forming character in children is not as simple as "A-B-C"! Those of us who work professionally in the process love to reduce the character formation process to lists of traits or sets of standard rules to respect. Organizing character into tables or lists helps us see it in smaller parts.

However, all the parts must go together *under* stress to produce strong character. Our academic respect turns to fear when our first child comes under our parental supervision. The task to help a totally dependent child become a competent independent adult is formidable.

Daily journal entries of your experiences will both train you to be a better parenting supervisor, and later, will reward you for work well done! Both natural parents and other parenting supervisors know the anger we have felt when a troubled teen makes some wrong choices. But, behind it all is a love and joy of satisfaction known only to parenting supervisors when that same teen grows into adulthood with character. Love, because we were there during the good times and the bad times of that child's development. Satisfaction that comes when we are blessed to see the finished product ...a confident healthy adult, a person of *character*!

Discussion Questions:

1) "The process of organizing _____ and _____ _____ result in the formation of character."

2) According to the Bible, what is one result of children learning to obey parents?

3) Why do high skyscraper buildings sway? (To withstand the _____of _____)?

4) Discuss the various things that can happen when a person is under stress, or adversity?

5) Discuss the reality of "change in our world". How do some people cope with change?

6) Define "resilience". Why is this trait important in a child's development?

7) Explain how character changes, but does not change!

8) Are character traits lists important? How?

9) What could entries in a daily parenting journal mean to you?

Chapter 11

⋅⟶◈⟵⋅

CHARACTER:
The *Finished* Product!

PARENTING SUPERVISION PRINCIPLES

36 *Effective Parental Supervision <u>is</u> the difference in Character...good or bad!*

37 *Supervisors must replace themselves with New (and hopefully, BETTER!) Supervisors.*

38 *The Final Goal of Supervision is to connect the past to the future.*

Bill E. Smith was "my minister" at a very critical time in my youthful development. He not only took the time to talk to me, but he supervised many of my early moral decisions. Bill had a very friendly, sometimes even funny way of relating to us. He was a man of high standards and sterling character traits, but his frailty as a human being often came through. We all knew he held to strong values and made good moral decisions, but occasionally he would say something that was, well ... just wrong! For example, on one occasion he was talking about how Jesus "was led as a sheep to the slaughter; and like *a lamb dumb* before his shearer, so opened he not his mouth," quoting Acts 8:32. In Bill's attempt to

163

communicate more clearly to unread students, he reversed the phrase and possibly in a dyslexia-moment "dumb lamb" came out as "*damb lumb!*" (You can imagine the reactions to a group of young people on the second pew!)

Effective supervisors are human. You may *sometimes* say or do things that simply contradict the values and standards you espouse. This cannot be your regular habit, but it happens. Even though I earlier emphasized the importance of being a good example, and of having your values and your behaviors in *sync,* self-deprecation on some occasions is a powerful trait in parenting. Children living under the authority of supervision delight to know that their authority figures are real people. Seeing our flaws help convey the message that they too are human. Their miscues should not cause them to stop trying. The process of struggling with what's *right* and what's *wrong* is very much a part of character formation. We become who we are through the fires of trials and errors.

So, what does the *finished product* look like? Do we define a person with character simply as a bundle of desirable traits? How do we account for the incongruent behaviors and the bad choices that may be in a person *of character*?

TRAIN UP A CHILD

First, we must understand that *supervision* is the difference in producing a good finished product and a bad one...a person *with* character, or just a *character!* Training is the controlled process, under supervision, that forms true character. That process begins the day a child is born and continues until no more training is needed. You pick a time! The *give and take* of making choices about our behaviors may begin when a baby needs the mother's milk and learns the power that comes from crying. The process continues and is even escalates during the "terrible-twos", a time many mothers try not to remember. The A, B, C's become the P-Q's, then the X, Y, Z's as our choices and our consequences become more complex! The truth is that we are actually under somebody's, or some-kind of supervision as long as we live. Our character continues to grow and develop, but it maintains the basic structure of our early childhood days.

In those early *before school-room days*, it is important that the parental supervisors be PARENTS! Your child may have several friends, but you are the *only* parents. This is true for natural parents, but it becomes more complex for professional parenting supervisors. An *un-natural* parental supervisor must supervise the behaviors of the present, and the ineffective parenting of the past. Regardless, whether natural parents or professional supervisors, training younger children centers around parental authority and child submission. This approach is based on the following assumptions:

- parents know what is *best* and *right* (community values) more than children,

- parents must teach what is acceptable (right) or unacceptable (wrong) behaviors

- parents must convey the values, rules, and boundaries of the community to and through their children

From birth to early school days the word *"NEED"* is more important to your parenting supervision than the word *"LIKE."* The needs of a child must be provided by the parents. Your core relationship with your child is based on your ability to effectively be authoritative without being abusive. The basic lesson your child will learn is how to obey while developing self-respect. This process gradually reverses as the child grows older and his or her ability to make choices that are more congruent with community values. If the parental training has been both effective and administered with good supervision, as the child grows older he or she will begin to act independently of the parents. Various personal traits will become more distinct and clear. The tools for making good decisions are honed so that we refer to them as "sharp" children.

Over time a baby becomes an adult. The strings of good choices are documented with framed certificates on the wall. The fumbles and poor choices often become only a laughing matter when the family gets together. Milestones, like graduations, are marked with celebrations.

Parental supervisors both wipe their brows with a 'WHEW!" and their eyes light up with a "WOW!" as they witness *the finished product.* –A GROWN ADULT WITH CHARACTER!

HORSESHOES OR HAIRSPRINGS?

One of the illustrations I remember from Bill E. Smith is recorded in his book, *"Train ...up a Child."* Bill went to the hardware store and bought a horseshoe for $2.25. After buying the horseshoe he asked the man to weigh it for him. Then he went to a department store and bought a package of safety pins. They cost him 10 cents each. Finally, he went to a Jeweler's and bought a hairspring for a watch. It cost him $18.45. He had the Jeweler weigh the hairspring. He then went back to his office to compare the costs. His conclusion was: "If I melted down the $2.25 horseshoe, I could produce $300 worth of safety pins from the metal. Or, with the same amount of metal I could produce $40,000,000 worth of hairsprings"!

What made the different? All three products were made from the same metal? He concluded that the value of the product was determined by the *refining* it received. It takes a lot more time and effort to make a precision-built hairspring with just the right tension to make the watch run accurately for years.

Forming character in a child takes time and effort. Parental supervisors have the daunting task of instilling these foundations of society under very adverse circumstances. Not only do they receive resistance from the child, but often from other forces in the community. That's a big job, but the more time and effort you spend in doing it, the more valuable the finished product will be for our world. Parental supervision is the key both to effective training now, and for the finished product of the future.

SUPERVISEES TO SUPERVISORS

What do we want the *finished product* to look like and why? The formation of character is an unending task for all of us. That we understand. We know we will be practicing our A-B-C's for a lifetime as we face challenges and make choices based on our values. The *Acceptable behavior choices* system is not only the process of forming character; it is the framework for building a life. We probably should not talk about character as "the finished product" as if looking in a rear view mirror. However, maybe there is value, as we supervise, to visualize a model of what the "child" *should ideally* become when and if that child forms *good character*. This model that follows neither includes all the traits of a complex character, nor does it purport to fit all cultures. I do believe it is a valid working model for training children to live in a typical American Judeo/Christian community. It does give us an image of what we should expect to see as a result of our supervision.

So, the following seven-point description is provided to visualize a working model of *the finished product*. This description could *characterize* how parental supervision effectively makes a difference in what a child *is* and what a child may *become*!

1 - LEARN OBEDIENCE AND BE HUMBLE

Our world functions by law, - man's and God's! We all understand the laws of nature which must be obeyed. If you fall out of an airplane without a parachute, by the laws of nature, you will die. Thus, we submit ourselves to the buckles and restraints of the 'chute so that we can live. Who of us has not known the concern we felt when we saw a blue light in our rear view mirror. It made us quickly look down to see if our seatbelt was buckled and the speedometer was within lawful limits. Just a few experiences like these call us to our senses and humbles our spirits.

Learning to *obey the law* (of God and man!) is an important part of successfully living in our communities.

Learning to *obey* both springs from *and* produces humility. Humility is the quality or state of *not thinking* you are above the law or other people. It is a quality of being courteously respectful of others. Many of the laws that we must obey are designed to elicit our humility, being respectful of others. A zoning law will restrict you from having a hog farm in your residential neighborhood, ...out of respect for your neighbors. Submitting to the laws of the land (constitutional, state, county, city, sub-division, family!) teaches us to consider others. This is a major key to successfully live in a community with other people of differing ideas. A person cannot live peaceably with others and ignore the rules and boundaries of the community. A person must learn to submit in order to survive. Forming this trait in children is under the direct supervision of the parents. They know what is right and wrong and it is their parental duty, with authority, to convey that to their children.

Parental supervisors begin the formation of humility in a child by insisting that rules and boundaries of daily living are observed and respected. Good character is not developed when a parent allows a child to violate the rules and boundaries established by the family with impunity. This trait of character can only be formed by establishing (and maintaining) clear boundaries and understood rules.

Teaching obedience is the first task of parental supervision. It can be difficult and challenging, but the ultimate benefits are far more important. The resulting *humbleness* will not only make it possible for your child to function in a community by respecting others, but it will also cause others to *like your child!* The negative impact of adverse reactions of the community to your child's disobedience can result in emotional trauma for the child, ...such as low self-esteem, depression, anxiety, or even more serious adult mental disorders.

Humbleness, with respect for others, begins in placing restrictions on a child's daily routines such as where they eat, when they eat, a time to go to bed, and to get up. Other restrictions may apply to social events, recreational outings or team sports. Submitting (or not) to the rules and boundaries must be coupled with both privileges and consequences. Obedience is not always easily taught, and sometimes may be even painful. A child learns obedience in much the same way as Jesus ..."by the things which he suffered (Hebrews 5:8)."

Training a child to learn to obey is hard on the supervisors and the child, but it produces humility! Humility is not weakness, but strength! Respectfully serving others in a community of need places the child in a strong position. The truth is, humility is power. He who serves best, rules. Personal confidence, not pride, grows as a child becomes known as a model for others to follow. As noted earlier, "Be thou an example...!" Submission to the standards is not bad, but good!

2 - BE SELF-CONFIDENT WITH RESPECT

Our second descriptor of *the finished product* is to see steady growth toward independence through a healthy self-concept. We want to see a young person who is sure of himself, but has the respect of the community. Respect is a feeling of deep admiration for someone or something elicited by their abilities, qualities, or achievements. The ABC system is designed to both provide a platform for a child to act acceptably in the child's world, and a process of rewards and restrictions to allow choices that provide opportunities for achievements. The ultimate result is a free-standing, autonomous independent person making successful decisions about life. Self-confident and respected!

This steady march away from parental supervision is celebrated with more and more freedom. As additional wise choices are made, he or she is more respected by others that he or she will make good choices. The community, or family begins to see the pattern of good decisions, which results in the community awarding elements of leadership to the child. This is translated into better grades in school, graduations, and job promotions. In some areas of achievement there are medal, ribbons and titles. Like the little red engine, the child begins to believe..." I think I can...I think I can!" Self-confidence and community respect begin to grow at a rapid rate.

The emotions of a parental supervisor when these milestones are reached are similar to the feelings when the child rode his or her bicycle for the first time. We usually express our respect for their independent achievement with simple words: "I am *so-o-o* proud of you!" Yet, perhaps words of the song title "I did it my way" best describes the child's emotions.

A child's respect for others (humbleness) and his or her self-confidence which resulted in other's respect for that child seem to be incompatible. The truth is, pride is the opposite of humility. But, in a person of character a strong sense of self is attractive when humility is also obvious. Our *finished product* is strong *and* loving. *Firm* and *flexible!*

3 - DEVELOP INTEGRITY WITH SINCERITY

The third descriptive term that defines a person of character is actually the garden in which all the other traits grow...sincerity and integrity! Sincerity is the quality of being free from pretense, deceit, or hypocrisy. Words like honesty and genuineness help us understand the meaning. The word used in the Bible for "sincerity" means "judged by the sunlight." A piece of pottery might be held up to the sunlight to see if it has any filled-in cracks. Another Biblical definition is "without wax". The custom was to bury the dead in tombs covered with hard clay. Over time cracks would appear in the tops of the tombs. These would be filled with wax and whitewashed. Thus the term "whited sepulchers" (Matthew 23:27) was used by Jesus to define "deceit" in the Pharisees.

Sincerity is a matter of the heart and motivations. It refers to purity, unmixed candor between the behaviors that are external and the motivations that are internal.

Parental supervisors must continually call their children out for this comparison. If a person's motivations are not congruent with his or her actions, then there is deceit and hypocrisy. Integrity refers to the *oneness*, or unity of our lives. People of integrity have actions and hearts that are together...no deceit, no hypocrisy! In its most basic sense, integrity means to live out your life in private in the same way you live (or talk about) your life in public. In a more street-wise sense, "you are what you are!"

Integrity brings our values, motivations, actions and interactions together. Character is much more than isolated traits or worthy actions. Character is the whole person, as a *whole* person, *acting right* and motivated by a pure heart.

4 - PRACTICE LOVE OUT OF COMPASSION

Practicing love out of compassion is our fourth descriptor of the *finished product*. The Bible places "love" as the greatest character trait among the greatest! This composite virtue embodies so many of the values we want to see in our *finished product*. Love is the power that makes it possible to live in a community with others. Take note of the communal connections in these phrases:

love suffers long and is kind; love does not envy;
love does not parade itself,
(love) is not puffed up;
(love) does not behave rudely,
(love) does not seek its own;
(love) is not provoked,
(love) thinks no evil;
(love) does not rejoice in iniquity,
*   but rejoices in the truth;*
(love) bears all things, believes all things,
*   endures all things, hopes all things.*
Love never fails(1 Corinthians 13:4-8a).

Our children experience the joy of rewarding relationships when they learn to love. They know what it means to "give and take" in a marriage, or on the job, or with a neighbor next door. Love may be defined as a "strong feeling of affection and concern toward another person, as that arising from kinship or close friendship." A child must develop healthy relationships with others to succeed in today's world. Love is the powerful feeling and practice that makes this possible.

Compassion may be defined as a feeling of wanting to help someone who is sick, hungry, in trouble, etc. This trait probably springs from our own sense of need. Love with compassion produces a life of service toward others. We want our children to become true social servants who step up when needed to help others. We want them to be the first to volunteer when our security is threatened, and the last to leave when an emergency is called. These are people who care for others, ...and show it!

5 - BE RELIABLE WITH RESPONSIBILITIES

Fifth, our *finished product* is a reliable person whose integrity and motivations are transparent. This person acts responsibly without guidance or supervision. You can trust them. They are dependable. They follow through on obligations and duties. They have character within and could not act otherwise with their integrity.

Harry S. Truman is credited with the saying, "the buck stops here" in placing blame. He understood that the more responsible a person was, the more he or she could be blamed. This is the negative side of training a child to be responsible. Those "in charge" must bear the blame. However, being responsible and taking responsibility for the things that may go wrong are admirable character traits. We all dislike dealing with people who are irresponsible or who blame others. So being responsible is a character trait we desire for our children. Such a child will develop a good reputation. In addition, reliability is a trait that produces a strong self-esteem. Not only do others speak well of such children, but they also feel better about themselves.

6 - COMMITTED BY FAITH TO BE RESILIENT

Resilience is the capacity to recover quickly from difficulties. Resilience is character toughness. Resilience is our ability to stand under stress and catastrophe, then recover. Resilience comes from good and bad choices that resulted in improved choices over time. That's a convoluted way of saying: "They learned their lessons!"

It is fostered by supportive relationships with parents, peers and others, as well as maintaining basic beliefs and values that help people cope with the inevitable problems of life.

We want our children to surround themselves with people who will listen to them and be there for them in troublesome times. The ability to seek and accept help from others actually strengthens resilience. Such support can come from friends or family; but other relationships in civic groups, social clubs and places of worship provide opportunities for support. Volunteering to help others also builds resilience.

A child's faith is the backbone of his or her ability to stand during times of stress. The Bible contains a clear definition of faith: "Now faith is the assurance of things hoped for, the conviction of things not seen (Hebrews 11:1)." Simply put, the biblical definition of faith is "trusting in something you cannot explicitly prove." Faith is being committed to a cause, and acting on that commitment. Commitment is a noun that means the act of binding yourself to a course of action. Making a commitment involves dedicating yourself to a course of action.

Our desire for our children is that they become faithful souls! Faithful to their basic values and standards! Faithful in performing their duties to God and men! Faithful to trust that was instilled by their parenting supervisors to be the best they could be!

Faithfulness is to be *full* of *faith.* Faith is demonstrated by actions, behaviors that are lived-out in a way that others can see. A person of character stands or falls based his or her commitment to values.

7 - LIVE AN INSPIRED LIFE WITH A VISION

Finally, our *finished products* will be inspired by a vivid vision that will set them apart to truly make a difference in our world. Supervising the formation of character in a child is the exciting task of igniting a spark in the heart of a child that can change the world. This is the reward for those of us who parent such children. Effective parenting supervisors will see this potential in every child under their oversight. We instruct, train, discipline and encourage each child *as if* that child was going to become the ideal *finished product. The very best of the best!*

THE SUPERVISORS

Each generation builds on the shoulders of the last. Each of us as parenting supervisors have spent a lifetime establishing, refining and maintaining our values. There are some "truths" that are "self-evident", but others must be learned. Parents are told to teach them, and children are taught to learn them. The tried and true will remain, while the false and harmful will change. That's the process and the product of this generation, and the next.

Civilization 101 teaches that each generation builds on the last generations, not just the one previous, but all of history! We are products of someone else, not all-together-self-made! Our core relationships with significant others molded our persona over time.

Yet, having said that, it is the duty of parenting supervisors to equip the next generation with *our* values and *our* standards. We pass on what we hold to be true. We commit our rules, boundaries, and variances and we expect faithfulness. Yet, encrypted in our values is the mandated rule that they must decide for themselves! Yes, we trust that those who have received the commitments will act responsibly, now and in the future.

Our task as parenting supervisors is to give our children what we have, and to trust them to use it wisely.

⚜

An old legendary story may illustrate what the outcome of our work as parenting supervisors could be:

An old Indian father wanted to test the prowess of his three sons. In truth, he also wanted to test whether or not he had done a good job as their father. He pointed to a mountain, bold against the sky, and told his three sons to go climb the mountain. To go up as high as they could possibly go!

The three sons set out toward the towering mountain. The father knew their journeys would be challenging, and sometimes dangerous. All three sons, whose training had all come from the same father, competitively set their goals to ascend the heights of the mountain. Each was determined to return to the father and to present to him a token of how high up the mountain he had climbed.

After a few days, the first son returned carrying a rare white flower. The father knew this flower grew only at the timberline and nowhere else.

Some days later the second son returned with a hard red flint rock. He had gone above the timberline. There was no vegetation, just rocks. These first two sons brought back proof of how high they climbed.

After many days the third son returned. He told his father,

"I come back empty-handed! Where I went it was all snow and ice, nothing I could bring back! But, he continued, I stood and looked out over a vast valley where two mighty rivers flowed side-by-side then came together into a large body of water. It was the most beautiful sight I have ever seen!"

Weeping, the father knew this son had reached the summit.

"You may have come back empty-handed, but what you now have is more important than that, you now have a vision in your soul."

The ultimate goal of effective parenting supervisors is to produce parenting supervisors! The *finished product* of our work of supervising the formation of character in children should look very much like we look, ---*but better!*

Discussion Questions:

1) What have you learned from reading this book?

2) How will the information you have gained benefit you as a parenting supervisor?

3) Why do you think some supervisors are successful while others seem to fail?

4) How important is it to see parenting supervision as a ministry or mission in life?

Gresham R. Holton

Epilogue:

The Ideal Model

PARENTING SUPERVISION PRINCIPLES

39 *Jesus Christ is an ideal model for character formation for children to become responsible adults.*

40 *The ideal character formation plan is actually one that is <u>learned</u> and <u>lived.</u>*

Supervising the development of character in youth is not easy. The task is difficult because of the generation gap between the parenting supervisors and the aspirations of a new generation. Supervisors seek to maintain the security and safety of their current world. Youth naturally resist the *status quo* and opt for a different future. Effective supervisors see the resistance as on opportunity to strengthen the resilience of the youth's character instead of just correcting defiant disobedience. Our goal for the youth is always *independence*, or, the freedom to act and the ability to perform responsibly over the long haul.

The ABC system is presented as one method that can be effective in building character in children. We have openly stated, not as an apology but by way of explanation, that it is based on the Judeo-Christian traditions found in the Bible. It was developed over three decades in a Christian child care agency. The supervisors involved, and the training protocols they used were firmly based on Christian principles. Target goals (tags) and character traits were drawn from Christian values. When the children's training was over, they were expected to take their places in a culture and society largely governed by laws based on the Judeo-Christian standards.

The term "Christian" as used in this treatise is not so much a religious approach as it is a composite framework for character formation. As stated earlier, this book is more concerned with the *process* of forming character rather than the *content*. However, having said that, I trust that it is evident that the content is very important!

Thus, it should not be a surprise that the example of Jesus Christ is the ideal model. His basic traits and values are central in this training approach. This character information is largely found in the Gospel records of Matthew, Mark, Luke, and John of the New Testament. A cursory review of both the content of His character and the process he used in forming it in his disciples is a workable outline to summarize the Acceptable Behavior Choices approach.

HIS CHARACTER EMERGING

The Jewish traditions focused on training children at a very young age. Teaching the basic values of the culture involved daily training (Deuteronomy 6). Young Timothy is an example of that training (1 & 2 Timothy). Timothy's mother (and grandmother) taught him. In the last letter from the apostle Paul to Timothy, he is told to be strong in the face of coming adversities. He was warned to "guard what was committed" to his trust (2

Timothy 6:20).   Jesus must have been trained in the same way.

There is not much recorded in the New Testament about the youthful years of Jesus. We know some of the things about the first eight days of his life on earth, but very little otherwise. We do know that he spent some time in Egypt and grew up in Nazareth learning the trade of carpentry.

The Gospel of Luke records that by the age of twelve Jesus demonstrated the ability to stand up with the fathers of his age. A detailed account (Read chapter 2) of one such event is recorded by Dr. Luke on a trip with his parents to Jerusalem to celebrate the Passover.   His parents found him in the temple conversing with those in the temple "listening to them" and "asking them questions (Luke 2:46)."

Jesus already had an inner strength of character that propelled him into an independent stance even while separated from his parents. He "grew and became strong (Luke 2:40)." He was filled with wisdom and the Grace of God was upon Him. The marvelous part of this story is that "all that heard Him were astonished at His understanding and answers (Luke 2:47)."

The adults listening to Him in the temple must have believed that He was taught and understood *what they understood* to be reality in their culture.   There is no indication of opposition, but to the contrary, they appeared to be impressed with his understanding. Perhaps he had been taught well by His mother! Or, possibly by His Heavenly Father!

The parenting supervisors of Jesus (his "foster" parents) saw the event as an act of disobedience. Those of us of faith reading the passage today see it as a result of His inner strength and character. Jesus correctly expressed what He was about *at that point,* at that age, but much more was to come. He understood who He was, and had his priority goals right, but growth was still predicted (Luke 2:51-52):

> *51 Then he went down to Nazareth with them and was obedient to them. But his mother treasured all these things in her heart. 52 And Jesus grew in wisdom and stature, and in favor with God and man.*

The character of Jesus became very visible in the short three-plus years recorded as an adult. He was a "man of sorrows" weeping at the death of his friend, Lazarus; and he was the authoritative voice that drove the money-changers out of the temple! He was the gentle "lamb of God" and good shepherd, but he confronted the highest authorities of his day. The unending love of Jesus accepted in his circle of influence men who loved him (John) and others he knew would betray him (Judas). He had the very authority of God to literally call down angels, but he controlled his actions for the greater good. He paid his taxes although he claimed citizenship in another world. The respect for the past was openly stated, although he pointed his followers to the future.

Jesus Christ literally changed the world! This, not in spite of, but *because* of his ability to submit and obey. Such submission was not always easy. He had rather let the "cup" of suffering pass from him. He was strong when he was weak. His character carried him through the troublesome years of supervising the development of character in his close disciples, the apostles. The content of His character is the ideal model for Christian parenting.

The passage in the second chapter of Luke suggests seven principles that form an outline using Jesus as our

"Ideal Model".   Reviewing those principles will help you summarize *The ABC's of Effective Parenting.*

1) Character development is a lifelong growing process.

The record says Jesus *grew* in wisdom.   The Bible teaches that Jesus was God's son ...but, more than that, Jesus was *God!*

Jesus *GREW!*? This basic belief of Christianity forces us to ask, "How was it possible for Him to grow in wisdom?" We can understand how his "stature" could grow as his human body matured, but how could God get wiser?

Perhaps this is a signal to us that at the age of twelve Jesus began the process of becoming spiritually and physically ready for His mission in life.   No one would argue that the mission of Jesus was just to be a child, but to the contrary, he was to grow to manhood and to literally change the world! It had been ten or twelve years since the last references to Him as a baby. It will be more than twelve years before we next see Him coming to be baptized by John. Following that, there were three very intense years of his public ministry in which he called and trained his small band of followers.   These years ended with His tragic appointment in Jerusalem and death on the cross.

For our benefit, all along the way images of His character immerge. At first it was through the angels of heaven who heralded his birth or the wise men from the East who spoke of his kingship.

On this occasion, the astonishment caused by the questions and answers of a twelve-year old boy in the temple!   Mary, his mother, might have shared the thoughts that "she treasured in her heart (Luke 2:51)" about her son with others. Here a little and there a little, the character of Jesus immerged for public view.

Finally, we are all privy to more than three years of interactions with his friends and foes, the rich and the poor, men and women those who challenged Him, loved Him and betrayed Him. We are blessed to read about hundreds of teachable moments in the life of the Master. Jesus gave us the example of what a *good character* looks like in perfection ...and, how it relates to others!

The point: If the very Son of God "grew" in wisdom and favor with God and man, then why should we think it strange to grow in the same way?

Character can change over time, for the better or worse! Adversity and failure (or, success and achievement!) can make us stronger or weaker. Through the Grace of God character can change! Although the formative years of youth are critically important in character formation, it actually takes a lifetime.

2) Developing character is a social interaction process.

Imagine a twelve-year old boy standing before the city's fathers asking questions and listening! *In the temple,* no less! More amazing, they were astonished at his answers! Jesus made a major impact on those in the temple with His wise and prudent remarks. His decision to stay behind after His family left showed independent thinking. In addition to that, this incident suggests His mother a clear picture of the ultimate goal of parental supervision... *independence.* She saw something in her son that was destined for bigger things than just being her boy.

Character is chiseled out by our rapid-fire interactions with others over time. Our behavior choices are constantly being monitored by others around us, especially our significant others. We receive feedback on our choices as "acceptable" or "unacceptable" based on the social norms of the group. Violations of those norms, or bad choices, result in disciplining actions administered by our parenting supervisors. This interactive process results in the formation of a framework for making behavior choices *within the values of our community.*

However, in the case of Jesus, his inner strength gave him the power to actually change the conventional values of his community!

I am not proposing Jesus *learned* his character from others. God's Son brought his deity with Him from the Father.

I am suggesting that the *process of His interactions* reveal how social interactions impact our mental, social and spiritual development. The actions and reactions of others who came in contact with Jesus demonstrate the importance of such social impact...*Jesus is our ideal model.*

Appendix

---·&·---

Case Study 1 – Making Acceptable Choices

Karla is a 17-year-old Hispanic female. Karla had been in several foster homes and numerous group homes throughout her life. Though Karla had a history of self-harm behaviors (cutting) and of chronic runaway, she had not exhibited those behaviors in several years.

In her survey, she indicated that getting a job and earning her own money was very important to her to be able to go shopping. She disliked any restrictions. She expressed that she was skeptical about being placed in this program as she was too old to have to be placed in a group home with a leveling system.

Karla's practical goals focused on her preparing for independent living.
1. Participate in job readiness training
2. Obtain employment
3. Open a bank account

Following the initial staffing with these goals set, Karla was optimistic about her success in the program. Each goal had numerous objectives. Karla participated in job readiness training and after several applications and interviews at various places she was able to obtain employment. Goals 2 and 3 required Karla to obtain a GA ID which required her to have her original Birth Certificate. Obtaining this document through no fault of Karla took considerable time to obtain.

However, Karla continued to make bad choices for her conduct. So Karla ran away. Her whereabouts were unknown for two days. She was located by law enforcement and returned home to Raintree Village.

Emergency staffing was granted by the Executive Director. Karla was placed back in the ABC system on Level 3. On her following staffing, Karla expressed that she hated being on Level 3 mainly because it meant that the houseparent was constantly near her. (The lower level a child is placed in the system, the more intense is the parental supervision.) In her words, "I felt like a child." She was feeling some of the "heat" being turned on by the ABC system. Her future is a matter of her choice. She could either begin to make good choices and have the restrictions removed, or her bad choices would continually cause her problems.

Karla began to make good choices. She eventually met her initial goals and moved up through the levels of the ABC system. This time Karla accepted life at Raintree Village and stayed for three years. She learned to make more acceptable choices for her behavior, and by the time she left, she was able to move to Level 10 during that time, the highest level of the system.

Case Study 2 – Behaviors and Training Levels

Nichole was referred to Raintree Village by the Department of Family and Children Services. She came into care in July of 2008 and was placed at Raintree Village in August of 2009.

She was removed from her mother's custody due to her mother's boyfriend making sexual advances toward Nichole. Numerous efforts were made to place Nichole with various family members but were unsuccessful.

Nichole is a 15-year-old African American female with a history of sexual and emotional abuse. The following can be said about Nichole:

1. Raised primarily in a single parent home.
2. Her mother struggled with a drug addiction.
3. She is the youngest of four siblings.
4. Initial assessments indicated her full scale IQ as 99. Her diagnostic impressions as: Axis I: Oppositional Defiant Disorder, Adjustment Disorder with Anxiety and Depressed Mood. Axis II: Antisocial traits/values, paranoid personality features. Axis III: Asthma (by history)

Nichole reported that though she hated school, she loved to read. Her favorite food was pizza and chicken wings. She stated that she loves to play basketball, likes going to the mall, and hanging out with her friends. This information was valuable in planning her ABC profile in administering both rewards and restriction.

At school, she exhibited the following behaviors: refusing to complete class assignments, inappropriate dress, and fighting with peers. But, she excelled in Language Arts and did not demonstrate any inappropriate behaviors in this class. At home, the following behaviors were observed: refusing to comply with directions such as to take a bath, to make bed, etc.

and verbally argumentative with her supervisors. She completed her assigned chores and did well with interacting with peers.

She was placed on Level 4-Training with her first staffing set for 4 weeks with the following goals:

1. Decrease school infraction from daily to only one infraction each week.
2. To take at least one shower each day.
3. To make bed each day

Nichole agreed to work toward these goals. She moved up to Level 5 in the shortest time possible. In addition to the other privileges that came with Level 5 she could now try-out for the basketball team. This was very important to her, so her staffing date was set with the tryout date in mind. Good choices are easier if a desired goal is obvious.

Therapeutic services were initiated to address the trauma of abuse. Nichole was reluctant to participate in individual counseling. She did however do well with participating in group counseling. She expressed that it was easier for her to open up with her peers present because they could truly empathize with her experiences.

MOM reports were reviewed weekly. Child care supervisors were reminded to encourage Nichole by praising her progress in the areas that she did well. Her supervisors had to be reminded to teach, direct, and redirect daily and to not just record the infractions on the MOM report. The MOM report should have "plusses" (+) as well as "minuses" (-). In a weekly meeting with Nichole, she explained that she felt that though she knew she had not made her bed, since she was not reminded to do so, she had not. The parenting supervisors expressed that she felt that since Nichole had been told to make her bed daily at her staffing meeting, she expected her to do without further direction. Child care supervisors must be reminded of the importance of teaching and giving clear directions. Nichole's staffing meeting occurred as scheduled. Nichole, her child care supervisor, an additional staff, and the MOM report showed that Nichole had met her goals:

1. Decrease school infraction from daily to only one infraction each week.
    a. 1st week-teacher called to state that she was dressed inappropriately at school
    b. 2nd week-no infractions
    c. 3rd week-school administrator called to state that Nichole had been sent to the office for arguing with a peer at school
    d. 4th week-no infractions
2. To take at least one shower each day.
    a. Took showers daily
3. To make bed each day
    a. 1st week and 2nd week-made bed three times
    b. 3rd and 4th week-make bed daily

She had earned the right by making good choices to move up to Level 5 and to enjoy the privileges of that level. One of those privileges was that she was given the opportunity the following day to complete her sports physical and to begin basketball tryouts.

Nichole was at Raintree for over 2 years. In those 2 years, Nichole progressed to Level 7.

Case Study 3 – Administering the MOM report

Phillip was referred to Raintree Village by the Department of Family and Children Services. He came into care in April 2011 and was placed at Raintree Village in May 2012. He and his five siblings were removed from their mother's custody due to neglect and inadequate supervision.

Phillip is a 12-year-old Caucasian male. The following can be said about Phillip:

1. Though in the one year prior to him being placed State custody he was raised in a single parent home with his mother, the majority of his life he was raised with both father and mother, until father's untimely death.
2. He is the middle child of five siblings.
3. Initial assessments indicated his full scale IQ as 99. His diagnostic impressions as: Axis I: Neglect of Child, ADHD, Learning Disorder, Adjustment Disorder with Mixed Disturbance of Emotions and Conduct. Axis II: Low Average Intellectual Functioning. Axis III: No medical conditions reported. Axis IV: Foster Care-Group Home
4. Phillip participated in individual counseling and was prescribed a medication for ADHD.

In first meeting with Phillip, he was initially reluctant to talk or ask questions. He had a hard time staying seated. Instead, he opted to stand up or crawl under the table. Though he refused to complete the initial survey on his own, he agreed to answer the questions as long as he did not have to write himself. He voiced that he likes to go fishing and hunting. He likes eating sweets and ice cream (popsicles only). He hates going to the doctor, Social Studies, and talking on the telephone. His initial staffing meeting was scheduled and explained to him. He quickly replied he would never remember that date.

MOM reports indicated low score in Personal Care (care of body, care of teeth, care of hair, study habits) and in school conduct. Supervisors reported that he would often pretend to have taken a bath and brush his teeth. When redirected, he would try to distract from the direction by talking about everything else. Supervisors also reported that he denied having homework daily. Teachers called daily home from school reporting that Phillip disrupted class by talking out loud and that he had not completed his homework.

For Philip, in addition to ensuring that medications were properly administered, it was very important that he be provided a physical structured outlet, such as playing games outside and going fishing. He loved to play outside. More than any other influence, his play time determined the mood and the success of his day.

He began on Level 4 with the following goal and objectives:
1. Improve personal hygiene tasks
    a. Take 2 showers each day
    b. Brush teeth 2 times each day
    c. Wash hair 2 times each week

Several parent teacher conferences were held to work together with teachers to incorporate strategies at home with a behavior support plan at school.

In addition to the MOM report being completed, a chart was posted in his room that he checked off daily each time he took his shower, brushed his teeth, and washed his hair. Though he went outside every day, he was able to go fishing on Saturdays if he completed each task each day.

Phillip made significant progress in accomplishing these goals in about nine weeks. Phillips was moved to Level 5. During the next few weeks, Phillip was caught on several occasions stealing at school and at home. At his next staffing meeting, stealing behavior was addressed. Phillip voiced that he did not have paper and anything to write with. Though Phillip had been provided with these supplies, he was out and stated, "I just thought it would be easy and ok, if I took some from my teacher or from one of the other kids."

After some teaching about stealing and on getting needs and wants, Phillip was provided with supplies. Supervisors were reminded to check daily that Phillip has what he needs by not only asking him but checking through his book bag with him.

Child's Survey

ABC
Acceptable Behavior Choices

Your Name: _____

What Name do you want to be called by:

_____ _____

Your Birthday: (Month/Day/Year): (____/____/_____)

Your Age: _____

Gender: (   ) Female (   ) Male

Race: (   ) African-American
             (   ) Caucasian
             (   ) Hispanic
             (   ) Native-American
             (   ) Other
What grade are you in School: _____

What is your MOST favorite subject in school:
_____

What is your LEAST favorite subject in school:
_____

According to grades, are you:
             (   ) Very good student in school
             (   ) A good student in school
             (   ) An average student in school
             (   ) A fair student in school
             (   ) Not very good in school

YOUR "LIKES" SURVEY

<u>Instructions:</u> On the following "likes" questions, mark your rank from 1 to 10. On this set of questions "1" means you <u>LIKE IT LESS</u>, and a "10" means you <u>REALLY LIKE</u> IT!

THINGS I LIKE:	LIKE LESS............REALLY LIKE
1) Eating sweets	1 2 3 4 5 6 7 8 9 10
2) Playing baseball	1 2 3 4 5 6 7 8 9 10
3) Popcorn:	1 2 3 4 5 6 7 8 9 10
4) Listening to music	1 2 3 4 5 6 7 8 9 10
5) Choose my seat at church	1 2 3 4 5 6 7 89 10
6) Going for Ice cream	1 2 3 4 5 6 7 8 9 10
7) Playing video games	1 2 3 4 5 6 7 8 9 10
8) Watching television	1 2 3 4 5 6 7 8 9 10
9) Listening to radio	1 2 3 4 5 6 7 8 9 10
10) Talking on telephone	1 2 3 4 5 6 7 8 9 10
11) Earn money	1 2 3 4 5 6 7 8 9 10
12) Work off campus	1 2 3 4 5 6 7 8 9 10
13) Going to school events	1 2 3 4 5 6 7 8 9 10
14) Hanging out with friends	1 2 3 4 5 6 7 8 9 10
15) Riding my bicycle	1 2 3 4 5 6 7 8 9 10
16) Using Computer/Internet	1 2 3 4 5 6 7 8 9 10
17) Going Wild Adventures	1 2 3 4 5 6 7 8 9 10
18) Visiting with friends	1 2 3 4 5 6 7 8 9 10
19) Reading books	1 2 3 4 5 6 7 8 9 10
20) Going to movies	1 2 3 4 5 6 7 8 9 10
21) Receiving mail	1 2 3 4 5 6 7 8 9 10
22) Fishing	1 2 3 4 5 6 7 8 9 10
23) Swimming	1 2 3 4 5 6 7 8 9 10
24) Going to video arcade	1 2 3 4 5 6 7 8 9 10

Other Things you LIKE: 1   2   3   4   5   6   7   8   9   10

_____

_____

_____

YOUR "DISLIKES" SURVEY

Instructions: This series of questions is to identify your DISLIKES.
A "1" means you DISLIKE IT LESS, and a "10" means you REALLY DISLIKE IT!

THINGS I DISLIKE: DISLIKE LESS............REALLY DISLIKE
1) Eating spinach   1 2 3 4 5 6 7 8 9 10
2) Room Restriction   1 2 3 4 5 6 7 8 9 10
3) Sitting in assigned seats   1 2 3 4 5 6 7 8 9 10
4) Going to the doctor   1 2 3 4 5 6 7 8 9 10
5) Additional chores at home   1 2 3 4 5 6 7 8 9 10
6) Limited telephone privileges 1 2 3 4 5 6 7 8 9 10
7) Taking medicine   1 2 3 4 5 6 7 8 9 10
8) Limited television watching 1 2 3 4 5 6 7 8 9 10
9) Limited listening to radio 1 2 3 4 5 6 7 8 9 10
10) Limited cash to spend   1 2 3 4 5 6 7 8 9 10
11) Limited time to hang out   1 2 3 4 5 6 7 8 9 10
12) Restrictions on social outings 1 2 3 4 5 6 7 8 9 10
13) Restricted use of M-3, I-Pod 1 2 3 4 5 6 7 8 9 10
14) Restrictions on bicycle or car 1 2 3 4 5 6 7 8 9 10
15) Limited visits with friends 1 2 3 4 5 6 7 8 9 10
16) Limited use Computer/Intnet 1 2 3 4 5 6 7 8 9 10
17) Wild Adventures restrictions 1 2 3 4 5 6 7 8 9 10
18) School activities, restrictions 1 2 3 4 5 6 7 8 9 10
19) Outings, bowling restrictions 1 2 3 4 5 6 7 8 9 10
20) Going to movies, restrictions 1 2 3 4 5 6 7 8 9 10
21) Assigned seating at church   1 2 3 4 5 6 7 8 9 10
22) Recreation, restrictions   1 2 3 4 5 6 7 8 9 10
23) Sports, restrictions   1 2 3 4 5 6 7 8 9 10
24) Restricted Access to my mail, 1 2 3 4 5 6 7 8 9 10
Other Things you DISLIKE:

_____

Bonus Questions:
- Your Favorite FOOD: _____
- Your Favorite COLOR: _____

Form 2 –MOM REPORT

Child's Name:_____ ABC MODE:_____LEVEL:_____

Age:_____ Male Female Supervisors: _____Date: _____

Personal Care:

	MO	TU	WE	TH	FR	SA	SU
Care of Body							
Clothing Care							
Eating Habits							
Care of Teeth							
Hair Care							
Personal Appearance							
Personal Hygiene							
Physical Exercise							
Sleeping Habits							
Study Habits							

*BPS Score: _____

Social Responsibilities

	MO	TU	WE	TH	FR	SA	SU
On Time							
School Conduct							
Transportation Conduct							
Tutoring							
Dining Hall Conduct							
Communications							
Physical Violence							
Property Violence							
Sexual Conduct							
Church Conduct							
Property of others							
Internet/Telephone							
Safety							
Courteous							
Social Manners							

*BPS Score: _____

Family Duties:

	MO	TU	WE	TH	FR	SA	SU
Chores							
General Room Care							
Closet Care							
Bed Care							
Bed-time Conduct							
Getting up from Bed							
Night-time Curfew							
Respects Authority							
Other's Space							
Interpersonal Talk							
Interpersonal Conduct							
Meal-time Conduct							

*BPS Score:_____

Supervisor Comments:

*Basic Progress Scale Score (Section squares divided by pluses (+))
**Total Basic Progress Scale Score (All squares divided by all pluses)
***Average of all family BPS scores

**TOTAL BPS:____

***FFS Score: _____

ABC FORM-3

Staffing Meeting Sample

Purpose:

The Staffing Meeting is to review and evaluate the conduct of a youth during a previous time segment with the task to consider a move for a child from one Conduct Level to another. The results of the meeting will be either positive, or negative for the child.

Those in the Meeting:

The participants in the meeting include:
- the child or youth being evaluated
- the direct child care supervisor
- a social services case worker
- another staff member
- possibly another child, one on a higher Conduct Level

Scheduling the Meeting:

Routine Staffing Meetings are scheduled in advance based on the Conduct Level of the particular child. A calendar date is set with advance notice to the child so that preparations can be made. Occasionally an "emergency staffing" is required. However, an emergency staffing should never be used for routine infractions of the rules.

Conducting the Meeting:

One of the social service professionals will chair the meeting following a preset agenda. The agenda will be publicized well in advance so that both the child and the other participants will be clearly informed about what will be discussed. Minutes of the meeting will be taken by the other staff member in attendance and will become a permanent part of the child's case file.

Conduct Information:

The MOM reports will be used as the basis for the meeting. Other information may be brought by both staff members and, possibly, other children in care. Any "evidence" about the conduct of the child over the previous period may be elicited.

Decisions from the Meeting:

The social services staff, in consultations with the administration, will make the decision promote the child to a higher level, demote the child to the level just below where they were, or to maintain the child in the current level for another term.. The child should be given the decision of the staff within 3 days.

Philosophy for "Staffing Meetings":

These meetings are designed to do three major things:

1) To give the child a *fair hearing* on all matters that will affect his or her future. Sometimes situations are complicated by the fact that a child feels they are treated unfairly. Advance notice with an agenda for the meeting coupled with the addition of several "reviewers" (including another child) helps the child feel it is fair.

2) To *spread the "supervision" duties* out to several staff, particularly when the supervisory decision creates major problems for a child in terms of restrictions or punishment. This approach keeps the decision-making process more objective, rather than emotionally determined by a single supervisor. This also removes some of the negative vibes a single supervisor might receive from a child. His or her movement up, or down, is a group decision, rather than a single person decision.

3) Makes the process of movement from one Conduct Level to another *much slower and deliberate*. An overarching goal of the ABC System is help the child string good experiences and behaviors together over time. Slowing down the process enhances this goal.

Desirable Outcomes from the Meetings;

It is hoped that a child will begin to "look forward" to the staffing as an opportunity to "climb the ladder" to greater freedom, more rewards, and less restrictions.

The Mode of Maintenance (MOM) Report is the instrument used to determine the type of supervision required

Supervision Procedures:	SUPERVISION	ABC LEVELS
• Each child is placed under EVALUATION SUPERVISION, Level 4 on entry.	INDEPENDENCE SUPERVISION MODE	Time in Supervision (Ages 16-21) 1 – 3 Years
	Report-In	LEVEL 10: Independent Living
• 1st Staffing: Explain the ABC system defining the opportunities to advance.	MOM – 1/14	LEVEL 9; Seniors Honors
	MOM – 1/14	LEVEL 8: Regular Honors
• MOM evaluations are randomly made on pre-set days according to the Level.	MAINTENANCE SUPERVISION MODE	Time in Supervision (All Ages) 5 – 52 Weeks ®
	MOM –1 OF 7	LEVEL 7: High Maintenance
• Following a set Staffing Meeting, the new level and MOM report will be posted for all to see.	MOM –2 OF 7	LEVEL 6: Regular Maintenance
	MOM – 4 OF 7	LEVEL 5: Low Maintenance
• Child will be given a minimum and a maximum time to remain in a level before moving up.	EVALUATION SUPERVISION MODE	Time in Supervision (All Ages) 1-8 Weeks ®
	MOM – 5 OF 7	LEVEL 4: Training
• Decisions of Staffing can be: 1) **Move up** to next level 2) **Stay** in same level 3) **Move down** a level 4) **Discharge** from RTV	MOM – 5 OF 7	LEVEL 3: Discipline
	MOM – 7 OF 7	LEVEL 2: Restriction
	(Eye-sight)	LEVEL 1: Probation/Discharge

Resources

Attachment: *Attachment and Loss Volume One* 2nd Edition (Basic Books Classics) by John Bowlby (Sep 23, 1983) Tavistock Institute of Human Relations, 1969, 1982.

- *This is the ground-breaking work on attachment theory. It is a scholarly exposition of both the importance of relationships and the disorders that result in early detachment.*

Choice Theory by William Glasser, Harper-Collins Publishers, Inc., 10 East 53rd St. New York, New York 10022.

- *Glasser's work in facilities for imprisoned young girls initiated this study. The importance of establishing and maintaining internal controls through good choices is described. And, conversely, the failures of external controls are shown.*

First Things First by Stephen R. Covey, A. Roger Merrill, Rebecca R. Merrill Simon and Schuster, 1995.

- *This book builds on Covey's original book 7 Habits of Highly Effective People by focusing on the best use of our time.*

Reclaiming Youth at Risk: Our Hope for the Future by Larry K. Brendtro, Martin Brokenleg and Steven Van Bockern, National Educational Service, Bloomington, Indiana 1990.

- *These three Native Americans chronicle their work with troubled youth and the damaging effects of discouragement. This is one of the best little books available on helping troubled youth.*

Separation: Anxiety and Anger (Basic Books Classics,) Volume 2 by John Bowlby and Stephen A. Mitchell 1976.
- *The negative result of Bowlby's attachment theory is demonstrated in this book. The authors illustrate how many bad things happen when we become disconnected.*

The 7 Habits of Highly Effective People: Powerful Lessons in Personal Change by Stephen R. Covey
Simon and Schuster, 2013.
- *Covey, one of the first self-improvement gurus, lays out the basic personal organization needed to be effective. He helps us see the importance of quality in our choices.*

Uncommon: Finding Your Path to Significance, by Tony Dungy and Nathan Whitaker, Tyndale House, 2010.
- *This highly successful coach illustrates the importance of character in young people in this easy read. Basic values are shown as clear indicators of character, especially for athletes.*

Train...up a Child by Bill E. Smith, Helm Publishers, Oklahoma City, Oklahoma 1996.
- *This is a book written for young people, but the lessons it contains on parenting are solid. As a minister for more than half a century, Bill Smith approaches the injunctions in Proverbs 2:6 with basic core faith. Christian parenting supervisors will bond with Smith's approach.*

Strategies of Psychotherapy by Jay Haley has been out of print for several years.

- *This book and <u>Problem Solving Therapy</u> (John Wiley & Sons, 1987) focus on the context and goals of family therapy. Both are excellent examples of using the environment of the client, including the power of the therapist and the client's family, to change behaviors.*

The Collapse of Parenting: How We Hurt Our Kids When We Treat Them Like Grown-Ups by Leonard Sax, Basic Books, 2015.
- *This focal book sheds light on the tremendous importance of parenting, whether natural or professional. Reading chapter 9, "Teach Humility" is worth the price of the book. Dr. Sax's approach dovetails with the "submissive" nature of the ABC System.*

<u>*www.FosteringResilience:*</u> Website featuring the work of Dr. Kenneth Ginsberg, MD, MS, Ed, a pediatrician specializing in Adolescent Medicine at The Children's Hospital of Philadelphia and a Professor of Pediatrics at the University of Pennsylvania School of Medicine.
- *He also serves Philadelphia's homeless youth as Director of Health Services at Covenant House Pennsylvania. The theme that ties together his clinical practice, teaching, research and advocacy efforts is that of building on the strength of teenagers by fostering their internal resilience. His goal is to translate the best of what is known from research and practice into practical approaches parents, professionals and communities can use to prepare children and teens to thrive.*

www.ingramcontent.com/pod-product-compliance
Lightning Source LLC
Chambersburg PA
CBHW070953040426
42443CB00007B/495